"I've died twice in my life. The first time was an extremely dark and unpleasant experience. A time I'd rather forget quite frankly. But the second time was when I had a full conversation with many enlightened Spirits on the other side. This was the death where I was shown the life changing benefits of creating conscious habits. To live a life filled with joy, love and peace... in all that we do, say, think and feel." CK

The Five Lessons of Life

A True-Life-Story of a Woman Who
Survived Two
Extraordinary Near-Death-Experiences

By Carrie Kohan

ISBN: 979-8-47349-457-0

A FREEDOM MASTERS BOOK
published by

FREEDOM MASTERS
—PUBLISHING HOUSE—

FREEDOM MASTERS PUBLISHING
HOUSE

Estr. Do Castelo 230H
Vila Mirasol, Sesmarias
Albufeira, Portugal 8200-385

The Five

Lessons

of Life

by

CARRIE KOHAN

TABLE OF CONTENTS

PREFACE

There are many things I've learned from my Near-Death Experiences (NDEs), but one of the strongest messages I heard repeatedly is…

"Love Thyself, Love Thyself, Love Thyself"

In this book, it is my intention to share with you how to love yourself from the deepest levels. How to feel safe. How to find your inner compass and discover your direction in life; and most importantly, how to live your authentic life freely… With an open heart, and independent mind.

I lovingly share with you here what I've learned from the darkest of days to the brightest of teachings and encounters. And I hope that by reading or listening to this book, you will also discover 'The Five Lessons of Life' and use them well.

I pray you will learn how to create your ultimate dreams and have a greater understanding of why you are here at this particular point in Humanity's timeline. Please practice these 5 Lessons and use this book as if it's your own personal 'Owner's Manual' for your Body, Mind, Spirit and Soul.

Update: We've listened to your suggestions and added the following as per your requests:
- We've double spaced in between paragraphs for those with Learning Disabilities.
- We've added blank pages at the end for notes & ideas.
- We've added an index on page 186, to find key words.

Enjoy the book as both entertainment and a learning tool. I look forward to you joining me on this adventure - let's begin…
Much Love and Light, Carrie Kohan

Chapter 1

Taking Flight

It was the early 1990's and I was at home packing and saying good-bye to all my roommates in our home we affectionately called the 'Hippy-Dippy House'. Even though I was thrilled to be getting married, my heart ached with sadness in saying goodbye to all my good friends and roommates.

I was beginning to get cold feet about saying "I Do" so quickly to Michael. My fiancé was a younger man than me, and I had only met him 3 weeks earlier. Yet, here I was... Engaged, packing up all my belongings and moving to another city. I was even leaving my job to join Michael in his business as the franchise owner for motivational speaker Tony Robbins.

I began to question things like, "Am I doing the right thing? Is this too fast? Should we wait a bit longer until we know each other better? Will his family accept me?" Michael comes from a good Christian family after all. And my family... well, my Mom was a survivor of the Native Residential Schools. I'm

Metis (French, Cree and Ojibwe). And I haven't been very 'Christian' in my life at all. I've done some things I'm not really proud of. My greatest fear was falling in love, and being told I'm not good enough for him, or his family. Michael's family seemed to be lifted from the pages of a Norman Rockwell painting, and I came from the other side of the tracks.

Well, no sooner did I ask these questions, then my heart began to feel a heavy sensation on it. It felt like someone was sitting on my chest and I couldn't breathe. It was June 1993, and I was still a young woman. "Could I be having a heart attack? Nah…" I thought to myself, "No one dies this early from heart disease, do they?"

I put down the last of the photos I was packing away and bent over trying to cough. I was born a sickly kid, and this was a little trick I had learned over the years. Coughing usually worked in stopping any arrhythmia attacks, or palpitations. However, I found it was working less and less these days. My heart murmurs had grown over the past four years. They had escalated after having a truly heart-breaking event at the age of twenty-four. I had a brutal abortion that nearly killed me along with our child… I can honestly say, I never wanted that abortion. It was devastating in every way.

So why did I have the abortion if it was so heart breaking? Well, it was a series of circumstances that pushed us in the direction of giving up our child. I was living in Victoria, BC with my boyfriend at the time. We had learned we were pregnant out of

10

wedlock. It was 1988 and not a big thing by today's standards, but back then… It was one of the worst things we could have done to shame our families. Especially given he came from an upper-crust British family from a prestigious community on the island. The news hit us like a ton of bricks! We discussed getting married, running away, or even the unthinkable… having an abortion.

My boyfriend's father made it extremely clear that if born, our illegitimate baby would be shunned for the rest of her life. She would never be accepted into his family on any terms – period! But I was determined to have our child. I begged my boyfriend to ask his Mother for her blessings. His Mom had been hospitalized for the past 18 months and was incapacitated physically, but her mind was still sharp as a whip. I begged him to go to her, "She'll understand I'm sure of it" I said to him in desperation…

Well, he left the next morning for his daily visit with his Mom, and when he returned, I was shocked with the words that came out of his mouth! He came stumbling through our front door and collapsed into a heap of sobbing tears on our living room floor… I ran to his side. He shared through his pain that his mother had died unexpectedly in his arms. He never got to ask her about our child, but thankfully he was there to hold her hand and say goodbye.

His family was going through so much pain after his Mother's passing that we decided to go ahead and abort our child. I know by today's standards this wouldn't have even been considered as the only option, but at the time, we didn't want to cause any more shame or trauma to his family. Especially to his father, who was absolutely devastated over the loss of his wife.

God knows I wanted to keep our baby. I had lucid dreams about this little one and felt I knew her already. I felt her in my arms. I knew her face. She was so cute. Blond hair with blue eyes and the sweetest button nose. During one dream, I was told her name. It was Penelope. Penni for short. And to abort her went against everything I knew to be right in this world... But I did it. I admitted myself into the hospital and went through the operation without him - while I had the abortion, he was attending his mother's funeral. It was a tragic day for all of us.

After the abortion, the hospital staff sent me home just two hours after waking up from my operation – even though there was so much physical damage done inside of me. I was bleeding profusely, but the nurse dismissed it and said that it's all part of the procedure. She said that I'd heal over time. I just needed to go home and rest.

My Mom brought me back to her home, where I stayed on her couch for the next 7 days – hemorrhaging and drifting in and out of consciousness. I was moaning in agony for what felt like an eternity. Pieces of flesh continued to come out of me for the following week, reminding me of the horror I had agreed to. I simply wanted to die, and in fact nearly did! I had lost our baby and now my boyfriend had left me as well. I was bleeding to death and really didn't care. I had lost my will to live.

My child's father and longtime boyfriend came just once to see me at my Mom's after our abortion. It was an awkward visit. When he saw me laying on the couch in such poor condition, he went as pale as I was! His sadness and guilt were tangible, and it was no surprise I only saw him a couple of more times before we broke up permanently. Oddly enough, I felt no anger for him. He had experienced two deaths that fateful day. His Mom's and his daughter's. I knew I couldn't look to him for comfort because he was as torn up inside as I was. I could only wish that we would both heal over time.

It was actually my mom and her constant care who saved me from bleeding out. Mom kept insisting I go back to the hospital. But I refused. Abortions had just been legalized that very day in British Columbia. I was the first operation that morning and many of the hospital staff were not pleased to be doing this procedure at all! There had been clinic bombings and death threats with riots in the streets… The community was divided, and it was made very clear to me by the admitting nurse to NOT tell anyone what I was doing there – for fear of retaliation.

My Mom brought me home and covered her couch in plastic. She then layered it with warm, comforting, clean sheets and blankets… She packed me with icepacks, and I laid in blood-soaked towels. I could feel her panic, but I didn't want to see another nurse or doctor again! Hell No! It was in their care that I was butchered like this in the first place! Thankfully Mom was highly skilled in holistic medicine, and helped me heal at home with herbs, ice compresses and lots of sterile gauze... Healing physically took a full two to three weeks, but healing emotionally? That was another story indeed.

During a physical exam many months after the abortion, I was told the most devastating news. The doctor sat me down and said, "There is so much damage and scar tissue inside of you, that it's likely you'll never have children again." I felt the floor give way from underneath me! I had always wanted children, and here I was facing a life without them. Over time I came to the conclusion that this was God's way of punishing me for killing our daughter. And I felt strongly I deserved it.

For the next 4 years, I went into a deep depression and began to drink heavily. I felt like an empty shell of a woman and thought about suicide endlessly. And with a weakened heart from the trauma of our abortion, I began to get chest pains on a regular basis. I knew I had to turn my life around completely. I knew that if I didn't forgive myself and my ex's father soon, I'd die an early death along with our unborn daughter. Plus, knowing my family's long history with heart disease, I decided to take these chest pains more seriously... Especially this one I was now having while packing away all my belongings.

Another sharp pain stabbed me deep in my chest! Immediately,

I came back from the memory of my abortion and found myself in the Hippy House, bent over in pain… I remember thinking to myself, "I'm engaged! I can't die this soon! I want to marry Michael, but how do I tell him I can't have his children?" With that thought, I began to sweat and tremble. I collapsed onto my bed and considered that I might be having a heart attack. I made a deal with myself that I'd have a nap and if the pain persisted once I woke up, then I'd go to Emergency.

Well, no sooner had I laid down and closed my eyes, did a HUGE sharp pain hit me! It was like a knife piercing right through the center of my chest. This time it took my breath away and left me gasping for air.

Almost in slow motion, I felt myself sliding out of the top of my head and leaving my body behind… I soon realized I was having an out-of-body experience! I lifted up, up, up, right out of my bedroom! Within seconds and no time to react, a HUGE brown bird came swooping down and picked up my Spirit by the back of the neck. The Bird's large wingspan began to pump the air underneath us and we rose higher and higher, leaving my bedroom and home behind. We flew up through the rooftop and into the sky! I can still hear the swooshing sound of the bird's wings as we flew up and into the light. I was dead for the second time in my life… but where was I going this time?

Heaven? Or Hell?

CHAPTER 2

ENCOUNTER WITH AN ANGEL

Just weeks prior to my second death, I kept getting a message in my dreams that a huge shift was coming my way. It felt like I had to change everything in my life, or else...

After my first death a year ago in 1992, I was scared straight and decided to turn my life around. I had quit drinking and bartending in the nightclub called Richards On Richards. I became a vegetarian and practiced meditation. I even moved from the party scene of downtown Vancouver to the Hippy-Dippy House in the beachside community of Kitsilano. But now I was being asked in these dreams and visions to change my life's direction yet again?

These visions were not something new to me - being Native I had premonitions and messages that randomly came to me since I was a child. It was something that was common to the members of our family. My Nana had a gift-of-sight, as did my Mom. I believe my dad was also gifted as a medical intuitive. My sister, brother and I all showed promise of being Seers just like our elders. But we all had different abilities.

Cathy, my sister for instance, was able to see those who had passed away. And she was forever having things being thrown at her by Spirits who were trying to get her attention. We got used to this, and most of the time just ignored it.

My brother Tom was the dog whisperer. He could communicate with animals and hear what they had to say. He also had strong insights, premonitions and was a master at healing. Tom was truly amazing - he had a knack of being in the right place at the right time, to save people's lives. I can't tell you how many people my brother saved in his lifetime… So many so, that the local police got to know him by name because he was first on the scene of so many accidents. While others stood by and took photos and videos at accidents, Tom would take action, and save people from the brink of death.

Tom would just feel a sudden need to go out for a walk or a drive and BAM! He'd find himself running to the aid of a robbery victim, or a car crash survivor. He was always pulling drowning kids out of ponds or pools. Even when he was dying from Cancer, he stumbled upon three car accidents in one day! In one of them, Tom saved a young woman who had been crushed in her car by a transport truck just outside the Victoria

General Hospital… She would have bled to death, but Tom quickly tore his t-shirt apart and made a tourniquet, which stopped the gushing flow of blood from her severed leg. The woman was unconscious at the time that my brother cared for her. She never got to meet who saved her. That was my brother's style. Tom would come home and tell us another one of his amazing stories – he'd pour himself a glass of Crown Royal and toast to another life saved today!

As for me… I could see, hear, feel and sense everything around me – both good and not so good. I could remote view as a 3-year-old and astral-travel, especially in my dreamtime. As a kid, I'd have moments where I'd just freeze and my eyes would kinda bug-out. This was because I was witnessing in my mind's eye, events that were about to happen. Quite honestly, I was an unusual child, but in our family it was relatively normal. For years, all three of us siblings would question if these were gifts we all had, or were they curses? Whatever they were, they were some of our family's deepest secrets that we shared with very few people, including each other – for fear of being judged or deemed nuts.

Looking back, some of my visions were becoming really scary as I got older… I think I began drinking in my twenties as a way to escape and numb some of these visions and the pain. It was an attempt to keep these images away.

Some visions were good however and guided me. They'd pester me until I'd finally listen to them and would take action.

A great example of this was in 1990, when I felt a deep urge to leave Victoria BC after my abortion... I instinctively knew I had to move to the mainland of British Columbia to start a new life. But it was a frightening thought, because that meant I'd have to sell all my properties, leave my family and friends behind, and move to the large city of Vancouver – where I didn't know a soul. I finally followed that inner push and once I did, the sense of panic and urgency inside stopped. I came to see that every time I'd finally listen to that little voice inside, everything would come to a peaceful conclusion.

In the spring of 1990, I arrived in Vancouver still feeling emotionally wounded. And over the next two years I sought comfort through my next two relationships. The first was with a young man named Douglas Oakey. The funny thing with Doug was that, if we had married, my name would have been Carrie Oakey. (still makes me chuckle) The second relationship was with Brady Williams – he was an athletic dare-devil; a First Nations man who seemed to have nine lives... It was through his family that I learned to read palms and truly be open to our Native teachings. Both relationships were a year in length and ended sadly. Yet to this day, I remain good friends with both of them, and am grateful they came into my life when they did.

Then came Eric. We met during my third year in Vancouver, BC. He was so young compared to me, but was a breath of fresh air. Eric was wiser and more mature than most men I knew at the time. I tried to forget that he was only 22, while I was 27-years-old. Our age difference didn't seem to matter much at first... but over time, it became an issue.

I had begun to spend more time at Eric's apartment than in my own hippy house. Even though we were basically living together and were very much in love, I began to feel a separation growing between us. We had different goals in life. Eric was a young, vibrant man and was just starting off in life; while I was ready to settle down and get married.

The realization that our relationship would never make it, began to haunt me. I began to feel it was time to change my life around completely – yet again.

Thoughts of taking a different path began to pop up all around me. From discussions with friends, to ads on the TV, or songs on the radio - but I ignored them all. I loved this young man and was scared to leave him. Even though I was being shown every sign in the book that it was time to move on...

Then one afternoon the message climaxed when a beautiful Angel suddenly appeared in Eric and my living room! Yes, an Angel! She was about 7-feet-tall, radiant and she came with this same urgent message that I had been given over and over again. She immediately began to tell me, "It is time my dear. It is essential that you return to your home today! You have a predestined journey you need to accept. It is different than the path you are trying to force upon yourself. You must act immediately and leave. Time is of the essence!"

I asked her, "What about Eric?" The Angel reassured me

saying, "Eric is on his own path. He also needs this. Both of you need to be apart in order to move forward. In time you will understand. It is as important for Eric as it is for you, that you both part ways today." The Angel added, "You need to return to your home this evening. It is imperative you be there!"

The urgency in this message was coming through loud and clear… If the Angel could have picked me up and delivered me back to the Hippy House, I think she would have, but it had to be my choice. I apparently needed to decide for myself to leave… and leave soon!

The Angel continued in her firm tone, "We've tried to speak with you many times in different ways and through different people, but you have remained where you are for fear of the unknown. This is an extremely urgent time. They are having council on you! This is the last opportunity that will be offered to you. If you miss this opening, your outcome will be altered forever more."

Immediately, I saw a vision. The Angel was showing me that by not believing in our possibilities and choosing the 'safer route', life was going to be much more dull for both Eric and me. I could see that we'd both have huge regrets later on in life if we chose to settle, rather than grasp onto what was possible. The Angel added, "This is your final opportunity to live the enlightened path you've agreed to walk – but you've been too scared to do so. We can do no more for you. It is time for you to make your choice." The Angel paused... then smiled and faded away.

I was left with my jaw hanging open! I remember crying out to the empty room, "Wait! What do you mean they're having Council on me?" I could no longer see the Angel, but I could hear her reply. She said, "They are deliberating on your outcome... It's imperative you act quickly! Your crossroad is about to pass by. If you are not independent and home this evening, you will miss a pivotal moment in your timeline."

I must say, I've had some strange things happen in my lifetime, but never have I seen a 7 ft Angel in my living room before! Especially one telling me to run like the wind from my boyfriend and to start all over again.

This message came with SUCH urgency it shook me to the core! I had to act quickly. So, I decided to talk with Eric as soon as he came home from work. When he arrived, I was afraid to tell him that I had an 'Angelic visitor'... so instead, I decided to tell him 'I had a dream'. I had an Angel come to me during a nap and she came with a message.

As it turned out, Eric was also feeling the same urge to leave me as well! So, we broke up that afternoon on really good terms. Grabbing all my clothes, I immediately moved back to the free-spirited Hippy House.

Even though I had been living with Eric, I continued to pay rent for my sweet little room in the communal house all this time. I guess deep down I knew this break-up would come and I'd need a place to go to.

So, with great excitement, I jumped into my car and headed back to the Hippy-Dippy House. My many roommates were pretty surprised to see me return 'permanently'. We all ate dinner together and got caught up on each other's lives. Myron (a Cancer survivor and my dearest friend in the house) said, "I'm so glad you've come home tonight Carrie, because we're having a meditation session with a Stargate Experience this evening. He went on to explain that the 'Stargate' was a 6-foot copper pyramid-shaped structure that had been channeled by a man from California named Prageet Harris. Myron added, "It seems to amplify energy like a vortex. And it's said-to-be incredible to work with."

We didn't know the facilitator, Prageet. He just magically showed up with this large structure, because he apparently 'felt directed to do so'. In fact, it was like a scene out of the movie, 'Close Encounters of the Third Kind'… Eleven people from all around the world just randomly showed up at our home! All of them feeling directed to come and be open to whatever happened. I remember Myron saying to me warmly, "I really think this Stargate thing is part of your path Carrie, and you need to be here tonight." I laughed and agreed saying, "Yes… I think I'm meant to be here as well."

After dinner, Myron and I joined this small group of strangers in the property's workshop space. There was virtually no internet back then, yet there were eleven of us who travelled from Greece, Italy, the USA, and Canada – all feeling guided to gather with the same purpose. (This truly is another book onto itself, because it was the very first opening of the 11:11 Stargate on June 3, 1993) It was life-changing for each and every one of us. Not knowing what was to come at first, we all sat in a circle around the structure and began having the most insightful and profound meditations... It was incredible! It helped me let go of deeply ingrained beliefs and past pains. And after several days of cleansing myself spiritually, I felt really clear. So much so that I decided to finally go for it in life! Miraculously – twenty-four-hours later, I met Michael... my future husband.

In such a small space of time, life seemed to be going in a totally different direction. Looking back, I can now see how the Stargate Experience opened me up even more to hearing and seeing my Spirit guides and Angelic messages. But never did I think I'd be dead just weeks after 'Waking up' to this level of consciousness! Especially with it being just days after meeting Michael and getting engaged!

But there I was... being lifted up out of my body by the big brown bird. He was holding onto me gently with his talons and together we were heading towards the light... The giant brown bird cocked its head and leaned down to tell me that it was taking me on a journey. I asked, "Where?" The bird replied, "I'm taking you to meet with the Council." Immediately, I thought back to the Angel's warning, and horror struck me deep inside! I began to cry. I was fearful this day of judgment would come. Tears turned into a heavy sob as my spirit-body went limp. The massive bird interrupted my pity-party and said, "There's no need to be afraid. You'll see… We're almost there."

The bird flew us through a series of radiant white clouds which eventually opened up into a huge, glowing, brilliant white empty space. We landed ever so gently. The bird lowered me down, placing me on the most beautiful and comfortable, soft, cloud-like chair. As I looked down to see what this chair was made of, the huge bird bid me good-bye and flew away - disappearing into the blinding white light that surrounded us.

I was alone… Or so I thought!

"Change Your Words – Change Your World"
– CK

CHAPTER 3

THE WHITE VOID

It took a moment for my eyes to adjust because it was so bright in this vast space. Not only was this place an overwhelming sensation for my eyes, but for my ears as well! This space was void of sound. It was so quiet, it was deafening… My ears were pulsating with a pressure that was unfamiliar to them. Yet, I felt comfortable because the feeling of love was absolutely indescribable. It was beyond love… It was heaven.

I looked down at the chair once again that I was sitting on. It had no legs and looked like a really soft cloud. Yet it was firm and warm. It felt so good to sit on because it wasn't just a plain old chair. It was emanating energy… An energy of unconditional love! While drinking up this healing energy that was now pulsating through my entire body, I looked up again and was startled to discover someone was standing right in front of me!

I was so shocked that I jumped at the sight of him! Immediately, I recognized this beautiful Spirit and his kind face. He was the same Spirit who stood by my side during my first death – just a year or so prior. I felt the urge to call him God, Creator, or Everlasting Spirit, but understood that he also went by so many other names as well. I thought to myself, "What name do I call you?" And to my surprise this radiant Spirit answered back telepathically – thought to thought. He said with such warmth,

"It matters less the name you call me, as long as you call my name."

It was at that moment I realized I was speaking with "God". He was a radiant and kind-looking man. Suddenly a sense of knowledge washed over me. I was being given an insight or a 'download' of information from Creator. I could see in my mind's eye an idea was beginning to appear…

It became clear to me that I was seeing "God" because I was brought up believing in "God" from having a Catholic mom and Protestant father. Even though both parents had left the church when I was little, I was given the images of what God looked like through both of their faiths, my Sunday School teachings, and my Bible Classes of course.

Looking at 'God', I also was given the insight or idea that if I had been raised Muslim, I believe I would have seen Allah. Or if I was Hindu, I would have been in the presence of one of their many Gods as well. I had an overwhelming feeling that 'God' was PURE Energy! And it was my own belief of what God looked like that was creating the illusion of the God-Source Spirit that was now standing in front of me.

I began receiving more images and feelings, and more 'downloads' were being transferred into my mind and Spirit energetically. I came to understand that Creator is creative!

I saw that God brings people together to a higher state of consciousness through many different experiences, faiths and belief systems. And all of these faiths have varying degrees of knowledge or gifts. None is better than the other. They just are... They are tools and instruments to bring us all to the same point. And that point is what I saw as the 'Spirit Song'.

So, what's a Spirit Song? I'm not sure, but I feel it's what everything is made up of. It is the vibration of sound and music combined. A song of (and for) the masses – that unites all in a vibration of love.

Does the Spirit Song have something to do with String theory? I'm not sure. I'm not a scientist... but it is the message of what I was given. And I trust that it will reveal itself over time – just like everything else has to date through quantum physics and current science.

The vast vision I was being given, expanded out even further... I was being shown that we are part of a huge labyrinth. Our mission is to help and love each other, as much as we love and appreciate ourselves. I then thought to myself, "The Beatles had it right. All you need is love."

Soon I could see that it's not just ourselves as humans we need to help, but it's all living and supposed non-living things we need to nourish and cherish as well. I could soon see, what we think of as 'non-living' things (like your chair or clothing) have a life-force as well - and are very much alive.

I then saw an image that once we all transcend through love, everything around us will dematerialize. I watched this vision as everything and everyone on this planet began to dematerialize and became pixilated...

All of a sudden, the Spirits that were in the 'non-living' objects, began to rise up along with all the 'living' Spirits as well! The chairs, tables, tv screens, everything in this illusion began to dissolve and human-like figures began to rise up from each object. It was their Spirit or Essence that was rising up. Everything on Earth began to lift up and out of their physical form, and the world as we know it dissolved in my vision. The message I got was that we need to value and be grateful for everything and everyone in our world. We need to love and support everything we see, feel and sense. This will not only bring us out of the 'endless loop' and transform us into a utopia... but it will also have a ripple effect that will stretch out into all cosmos, and extraterrestrial nations, forever and a day.

This may feel so far off or even impossible for some, but it is our collective path. With every step that we take in the name of love, we will come closer to this ideal outcome. It all begins with the choices we make at this very moment – here today. We just need to believe that this day of 'loving thy neighbor unconditionally' is not only possible but could also be the most powerful choice we could ever make!

I could see that our focus must start by loving ourselves first. Then loving our fellow man, animal, plants, and even insects. I feel our whole purpose here on Earth, is to make the conscious decision to light our own internal flame of love and the rest of our purposes will unfold with ease and grace.

"It all starts from within", I heard a voice say deep inside me... Slowly I drifted back from these thoughts and came back into the brilliant white room. I could see that God was still standing in front of me in this place I came to know as the 'White Void'.

I felt an instant bond with 'Him'. Again, I saw him as a 'Him', because that was what I was taught as a child. If I was taught God was something like a petit woman with blue hair, or perhaps a giant purple dog... I understand that I would have seen God these ways instead. The God I saw, was just as I had seen in all of our illustrations on Earth. His eyes and beard twinkled with a light that warmed my soul. It made me feel instantly loved and cherished. Creator was surrounded by an aura or energy field that danced with a brilliant shimmering light. It was breathtaking. Words cannot describe the love and beauty I felt in 'His' presence.

All of a sudden something moved to my left and caught my eye. It was another being! I recognized him immediately as Jesus.

He also looked very much like the images I had seen on Earth. Only he was even kinder looking than what I had ever perceived him to be. The best illustration I've seen of Jesus since returning from this experience is a painting done by Akiane Kramarik.

The first time I saw her painting called, 'Jesus, The Prince of Peace', I cried. I literally burst into tears, because THIS image was of the Soul whom I sat with. He was the man I came to love so much in the White Void. I remember very little of our conversations, but I do remember the feeling of love and compassion he shared with me. No words could describe the feeling of utter peace I had during our time together.

Looking now at both God and Jesus, I felt such a sense of inner peace… but it didn't last for long. Soon this blissfulness was overtaken by my own fear. I was so afraid that I was about to be scolded or punished for my actions back on Earth. This was my 'Judgement Day' after all. That's what the Bible and traditional Churches had taught me. "It was time to be accountable for my actions" I thought to myself. And I only had two options really...

1. I could be shunned by God and face the Dark-side again. (Like I did during my first death) Or...

2. Creator could show me compassion and take my wounded Soul in. Perhaps I could be healed and find that elusive place of unconditional love that I had been searching for much of my life.

As God spoke, I sat frozen in fear of what was to come next...

"The thing about death is - it's a reminder to the rest of us to live" - CK

CHAPTER 4

THE COUNCIL OF MEN

Having been brought up on a military base in the late 60s and early 70s – our schools had strict and fear-driven Bible classes as part of the curriculum. I ended up eventually rejecting the teachings of the Bible. Instead, I became a long-time atheist. I remember looking at both God and Jesus in the White Void and automatically feeling fear, because that was what I had been taught. Back on Earth, all my teachings in both school and church taught me to be afraid of God. Faith didn't feel so good, so I rejected it.

As a young woman, I didn't want to live in fear any longer, so I chose to believe God and Jesus didn't exist. I thought by having no faith in anything other than my own abilities, I'd never be judged by God or anyone else for that matter. Boy was I wrong! The Spirits I feared the most and tried to escape from, were now standing in front of me in the White Void!

Looking at both God and Jesus, I remember saying to myself, "Holy Fuck! You're real!" And to my surprise, they reacted and were amused with my thoughts. Which then led me to think, "Ah crap! You can hear my thoughts too?" They both nodded and God said, "Yes, this is how we will communicate (thought to thought). It's alright. You're safe. We want to speak with you. So, let us begin."

"Begin?" I questioned. "Begin what?"

Creator turned and began to move away from me. I looked over at Jesus for reassurance, but he just smiled and then disappeared before my eyes! When I frantically looked back towards God, He was no longer in front of me. Instead, He was now sitting directly across at the center of a very long, semi-circle table. It looked similar to the painting of the 'Last Supper' because it also had 12 people sitting at it – equally divided on both sides of Creator.

With Jesus gone, I got a little nervous. I found myself sitting at the middle of the table, facing all these people. It felt like a court room quite frankly. Clinical, white and all these faces just staring at me.

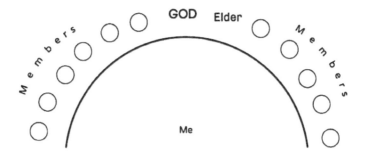

The Elders at the table were all male, and they were dressed in floor-length white and golden gowns. They had bright golden sashes wrapped around their waists, and they had a look of intense wisdom about them. God introduced the men seated beside him by saying, "Welcome. These are the Council of Men." I repeated the name in my mind because I had never heard of them before… "Council of Men?" I questioned. "Why are they all men? Where are the women?" The group smiled and God explained what I was seeing was an illusion of masculine energy personified as male figures.

God swept his arm from his left to the right bringing all of our attention to the empty vastness in this 'White Room'… He said, "There is much feminine energy all around us, but it is not visible to you right now. This feminine energy has a different, yet similar purpose than the masculine. The Feminine is often that of the Nurturers – and is part of what is known as the Angelic Realm. Their prime purpose is to answer the clarion calls. These Energies respond by sharing love, compassion, faith, trust, comfort, and many other qualities and resources to assist those who ask for help."

As God was speaking, I was downloading a vision at the same time. I could see all the prayers from people on Earth. They appeared as golden beams of light that stretched up into the Heavens. It was almost as if the beams of light were saying, "Pick me! Pick me!" Some beams of light were stronger than others, but all of them seemed to contain in them a request for help. Suddenly, I could hear voices within these light beams! I could hear each person's prayer. I heard a woman saying a quiet prayer under her breathe for her child; then another voice overlapped, as I heard a man praying for his child as well; then another voice was heard on top of the first two... This time it was a child who was asking for their parents to heal and to remain together. More and more voices popped up and soon it felt like millions of voices were speaking all at the same time. Each one crying out for help.

I looked closer and saw that these beams of light came out of the tops of the heads, as well as the center of the hearts of those people praying. Some beams of light were constant, while others were quick to appear and then they'd disappear. But what I sensed was each beam or 'light talk' was heard by an Angel and responded to. I was shown that many of those praying, felt they weren't heard. But every prayer was heard and responded to. Always! Not one was ever ignored.

In some cases, it would take years for the person praying to understand their prayers were in fact answered. Often what people plead for was not what was best for them. But in the end, I could see each person came to understand on some level that their prayers were answered... perhaps just not the way they expected them to be.

The visions also showed me that this was not considered 'work' for the Feminine (or Masculine) Angels. In fact, answering these prayers brought them great joy! I could see that we must ask for help before it can be given. And that prayers ranged from small to large. In cases of more urgent cries for help, I could see fleets of both male and female Angels coming to the rescue. They would team up and descend towards Earth at lightning speed in order to answer specific calls. But the vast majority of prayers were being answered by the Feminine from above. All these prayers were addressed almost as fast as they were received.

The images in my mind expanded again, and now I could see a view of the entire Planet. I noticed that out of all the millions of golden beams of light that were rising up from Earth – I could also see a small amount of green, pink and purple colored light beams as well. I was told these are prayers of gratitude, hope and faith. These people weren't requesting anything. They were simply feeling deep gratitude for their families, circumstances and lives. They were sharing with the heavens their deep appreciation. I could see that their beams of light were also being answered with even more gifts of love and appreciation in return.

Suddenly, God's voice interrupted the visions in my head, as he said, "You see, each Energetic Form here has its own purpose in assisting those in need. You are in the presence of the Council of Men, because you will benefit in healing the most from masculine energy. We are here in order to help you forgive and love yourself as much as we love you… We are here to show you that you are loved unconditionally. And it is our wish that you will learn to accept this love fully."

These Elders seemed to know me well. All I could feel was unconditional love coming from all their kind, smiling faces. With all this love in the air, it was becoming evident that these Souls loved me more than I loved myself!

God's face then become more serious as he said, "We were concerned about you. We've had Counsel on you many times. We witnessed moments where you were so lost, that we contemplated whether to bring you back or not – to save what was left of your Soul."

One of the Council Members then spoke up. He appeared to be the Head of the Council of Men. He introduced himself… I don't recall what his name was, but I felt he was an Elder. He asked, "Do you remember when you called upon us out of desperation for help?" I thought for a moment and then answered, "Yes, I do remember that. It was the first time in my life that I called out in the name of God for help, because I was truly lost."

My thoughts wandered back in time to the moment of my first death, just a little over a year ago. It was 1992 and I was 27-

years-old. I was drowning in such desperation and despair, that I finally stood up and pled to God for help! Never before had I believed in God or Jesus. I thought they were 'characters' created by the Church and a group of men who wrote the Bible. I believed the stories of God were an attempt by the original Catholic Church to control the masses. Whether this is true or not, I've come to realize it doesn't matter, because nothing is good or bad in Heaven – it just is.

My memory then shifted to a thought of my brother and me having a conversation together in our teens… Tom would often say, "Just look at all the wars in our world fought in the name of God or Allah! That's not spirituality! It's a man-made attempt to gain more control of land, power, resources and the people as well!"

I looked at God while finishing this memory, and then transferred another thought to him. I said, "So, I guess I never did trust in you Sir. I'm sorry." I added with a smile, "That was until I screamed out for your help of course, and miraculously, you showed up! Actually, both you and Jesus came and stood by my side. And even after that, I still didn't believe in you! I was ashamed to talk about my experiences. And I refused to believe that you even existed. Even though I saw both of you with my very own eyes."

The Elder of the Council smiled and conveyed the message, "We were happy you called for help. Some need to travel into depths of self-destruction before they understand who they are, and what they are capable of." The Elder added, "Often pain is one of the greatest motivators for change and is perhaps why many choose to experience pain first, before growth.

Sitting with the Council of Men, I could also see and feel that the answers to all our prayers were quite simple. I began to think about the beams of light again. I could see, feel and hear the pain in all those praying... These people were at their wits end. They were desperate for relief from their agony! Not understanding that their pain would be their catalyst for change. And if they would agree to step up and out of their current way of thinking, they could be free once and for all.

This was something that took me most of my life to realize. And it was only during what came next, that I truly comprehended that life didn't have to be traumatic or difficult any longer. Instead, life is what we choose it to be...

CHAPTER 5

MY FIRST DEATH

While sitting in front of the Council of Men and speaking with the Elder, my thoughts drifted back to my first death, and the origins of my own pain.

It wasn't long after our abortion, I began to drink heavily and spiral down into deep states of depression. On the outside I looked to have the world by the tail... I had moved to Vancouver and was working full time as crew on a long running CBC TV show, called 'Front Page Challenge'. I was also an up-and-coming actress and was on many TV shows like MacGyver and 21 Jump Street. I modelled petite fashions and had numerous national commercials with Disney, Mattel, Kenner, Tonka Toys, etc... I found myself always smiling for the camera, but on the inside – these were becoming the darkest times of my life!

Negative thinking and self-loathing thoughts about what I had done to our unborn baby seemed to be growing more and more inside me. And soon these low vibrational thoughts were attracting really dark and negative energies around me.

It started at first as a heavy feeling inside that I just couldn't shake. I couldn't get out of bed. I lived in my housecoat. I wasn't eating or sleeping well. I drank a lot of booze and ate a lot of junk food. Consequently, I had so many dark nightmare... This depression progressed and soon I was beginning to see things I thought at first were hallucinations. I could see black shadows zooming past me out of the corner of my eyes. I didn't know what they were at first, but I knew I didn't like how they felt at all.

Being Native or Aboriginal, we were taught as children to trust in what we felt, saw and sensed. As I said earlier, I had grown up seeing Spirits all my life, but these dark energies were different... They felt sinister! I discovered over time that these were 'Entities'. I learned later in life that there are good Entities and not so good Entities. Well, these ones I was encountering were definitely not good entities at all! I came to know them as the 'Shadow People' or 'Spirit Eaters'. The darker I personally became in my thoughts (especially while drinking) the more aggressive these Black Shadows became as well. Soon the Shadows were accompanied by two foot high, black, somewhat translucent, demonic-looking critters. I eventually came to call them the 'Gremlins'.

Prior to my first death, the Entities and Gremlins came to visit me nearly every night. Whether I was drinking or not. This went on for many months. They'd torment me as I'd try to fall asleep at night.

It seemed to be a cycle of darkness that I couldn't escape… I'd think bad thoughts, and the Gremlins would appear. Then I'd think even darker thoughts and of course more negative entities would come. This cycle went on for months! It seemed that the darker my thoughts became, the more excited and agitated the Gremlins and Entities would get. It felt like feeding time at the zoo quite frankly. However, I could feel the visits from these energetic parasites were coming to a climax. I knew that one day this would explode into a battle, and I'd have to stop it. The only thing was, I didn't feel confident or strong enough to fight them off. Their energy was STRONG! And I was outnumbered! I began to think, "I don't know how much longer I can last! This may be it for me…"

With money dwindling fast over the past two years, I went from renting one of the nicest 2-bedroom, waterfront, penthouse suites in the Westend of Vancouver, to eventually moving into one of the tiniest studio suites in the entire building!

Sixteen floors down I moved. And because I was still in the same building, it didn't surprise me when the demonic little Gremlins moved along with me. They were always in my apartment waiting for me at night when I'd come home from work ready to greet and haunt me…

I have snapshots in my mind about what happened the night of my first death. I was so drunk! I was beyond intoxicated. I remember a stranger driving me home that night from a party after work. He got me to my door and propped me up while he went through my purse – looking for the keys to my apartment. Once in, I remember him having to drag me to the bed where me placed me face up. I also recall being afraid he was going to rape me. But instead, he showed only kindness. He didn't want to hurt or take advantage of me. Thank God! He was extremely thoughtful and left a glass of water and empty bowl beside the bed – just in case I got sick. Then he left. To this day, I believe he was an Angel who was answering my prayers (or beams of light).

I was so inebriated that I couldn't move on the bed… So, when I began to choke on my own vomit, there was no way out but death.

I couldn't turn over when I started to get sick. I was trapped. As I choked, I felt no fear or pain whatsoever. I simply slipped out of the top of my body and waited for someone or something to come get me. But to my surprise no one did! There was no light. No kind, loving face, or greeting party to come meet me. No familiar relative to say, "Welcome home honey." I only felt a sense of darkness all around me. Instead of lifting up and leaving my body behind, I just hovered above my corpse like a lost soul. I remember being so cold and unsure of what to do next.

Prior to my first death, I had heard a little bit about Near-Death Experiences - NDE's. It was my understanding that people (especially good people) would go into a tunnel of light when they died. So why wasn't this happening to me? Other than my abortion, I thought I was a pretty good person. I had been an ideal daughter, sister and friend to many. I waited till I was 20-years-old to have my first serious boyfriend. I had never tried drugs. And I volunteered much of my youth in nursing homes. So, I really thought I was a good Soul and would go to heaven when I died…

The thing was, I just didn't like myself for what I had done to our child. In fact, I hated my ex's father! But most of all, I hated myself for what I had agreed to. Never did I think that self-loathing thoughts would be enough to destroy my Spirit! Never could I have imagined that my own self-hate and continuous fear-based thoughts would actually shut me out of the light when I died! But that's what happened… I was not going to Heaven. I was dead and in the in-between state – somewhere on the edge of Heaven and Hell.

Fear began to grow inside me. I was shivering from being so cold and really didn't know what to do next. But then it happened! The Gremlins began to surface through my floorboards – along with one of my greatest nightmares! A huge green snake!

The Devil whispers, You can't withstand the storm
The Warrior replies, I AM the storm" Anonymous

CHAPTER 6

TOE-TO-TOE WITH THE DEVIL

Over the past many years of telling my full story during our workshops, I'm often asked, "Do you really think there's a devil?" Well… I can only speak from my own experience and for me, here on Earth, I'd have to say "Yes!"

There's a Devil as much as there is a God, a Buddha, or Allah. We live in a world of contrast after all. We have an up and down; an in and out; a left and right; a black and white; good and bad; right and wrong… so if there is a God or a Light Energy, then we have to have something in contrast to this Light.

For me, at this time of our consciousness and evolution… yes, there is still a dark side, or what many would call the Devil or Satan.

I must say that I contemplated a lot about putting this part of my story into the book, because I wanted to focus on the goodness of the 5 Lessons of Life (which I'll get to soon, I promise). But from working with tens-of-thousands of clients in one-to-one and group sessions, I've come to discover many of them have also seen the dark-side. In fact, I'd dare say it's a common experience. Even more so today!

Many have had these experiences but choose to keep quiet about them out of fear and societal pressures. I believe it's time we open up and discuss everything Spiritual! Both Light and not-so-light. That being said, we do however need to focus ONLY on the light in order to move our collective consciousness into the next level of vibration and existence.

It is my intention to share with you here all that I know to be true. So, how do I know there is a Devil? Because when I died for the first time and lifted up and out of my body, I wasn't greeted by Angels and Divine Spirits. Oh no… I was greeted by the sound of evil growls and scratching noises that were demonic… The shrilling sounds were followed by the appearance of those little black gremlin-like creatures. They began to pop out of the floorboards again like a whack-a-mole game! The gremlins cornered my Spirit which was now floating above my corpse. They seemed to want to trap me for some reason. Well, that reason soon revealed itself…

A deep grinding and creaking noise began in the center of my studio suite. I watched as the living room floor opened up and fell away, revealing a gigantic, dark hole! This hole tunneled deep into the earth…

My Spirit and mind were able to quickly travel across the room and look down into this hole. I saw something large quickly moving up towards me! Screaming inside, I flew back and curled up beside my dead body – which was still laying on the bed in the corner of the room. This was not the reception I had expected after dying! It was my worst nightmare come true!

As I looked intensely at the tunnel in the middle of the room, I watched in terror as a gigantic green and black snake began to come up through the hole! I froze in utter fear! The snake rose up higher and higher until it was nearly hitting the ceiling! It was thick, shiny and MASSIVE! As the snake coiled its tail underneath itself, it reared up as if it was about to strike! Suddenly the snake stopped. It just stared at me as it flicked its tongue. He began to assess me. Trying hard to look deep into my eyes the snake began to sway side to side, but I instinctively looked away. I couldn't look into its eyes. He was too evil!

The snake suddenly began to jolt from side to side, as it began to shift and morph… It was turning into another creature right in front of my eyes!

My Spirit curled up even tighter in fear - hovering slightly above my bed as I watched this giant snake contort and transform into a man! A very tall, distinguished-looking man. Suddenly it dawned on me! I wasn't looking at a man... This was the Devil himself who was standing right in front of me!

Even though it was dark in my apartment, I could see the Devil's face as clear as day. Satan was handsome in an odd kind of way. Tall, dark, and muscular looking. He had a rugged square jaw-line, with high cheekbones. But his piercing cold, lifeless eyes were so difficult to look at... He had an intense sexual energy about him. I almost chuckled to myself thinking, "So this is where the term 'devilishly handsome' comes from."

Sensing I was trying to ease my terror through humor – the Devil became angry! He bolted towards me at lightning speed! I sensed he was attempting to gain control through utter fear. He never dropped his gaze. This lunge towards me made me jump! And immediately our eyes met! He had me...

I could feel my Spirit and mind being swept up in his intoxicating swirl of energy. His reptilian shaped eyes were hypnotic. They began to pulsate in an undulating motion, moving in and out. It was like I was melting away into an intense trance! He had control over me and was now diving in deep – in an attempt to rob me of my Spirit and Soul.

The Devil raised his hand and pointed it towards me. He summons my Spirit to unwind from the fetal position that I was curled up in. Immediately, I began to robotically move towards him. Together we drifted towards the hole in the middle of the studio suite's living room floor. He motioned for me to stop as I drifted very close to his face. There was no struggle. I was under his spell. Together we stood toe-to-toe. I felt so trapped and vulnerable, as we floated above the seemingly bottomless hole.

Looking into his eyes, I succumbed to his hypnotic energy which made me extremely sleepy. Just as I was about to drift deeply into the smoky grey fog that was beginning to surround us, I heard a desperate cry for help call out from deep within me. The voice was familir, and then it dawned on me! It was ME screaming inside myself! I was begging for my Spirit to WAKE UP! I heard my own voice crying out in anguish... Screaming, "NOOOOO!"

This cry for help was enough to shake me from the grips of the Devil's trance. I woke up and immediately took charge! I stepped back and instinctively withdrew from Satan both physically and mentally! My military training as a young air cadet was kicking in... I found myself standing to attention. My body was strong and erect. My chin was up high, and I was filled with determination. I was ready to fight and do whatever it took in order to win this battle for my life!

The soldier in me seemed to know exactly what to do. Instinctively, I called in an 'army' I had never considered I was even associated with before. Without hesitation I began to demand that God and Jesus be by my side! I remember thinking to myself, "If this truly is the Devil that was standing in front of me, then that means there has to be a God as well!" With this logic, I began to call out with everything I had in me, for help from above! I yelled inside, "God! Jesus! I need you to be by my side NOW!"

Instantly, not only could I sense God's presence to my right, but I also could see that Jesus was standing to my left as well! I was no longer alone in this fight. I had back up!

I didn't care if they were real or not... Maybe this was all a dream! Whatever it was, I was determined to win and be free from these demonic creatures once and for all! I wasn't alone in this battle, and that's all that mattered.

I can tell you that as soon as Creator arrived, the Devil looked terrified! I could see the fear in Satan's eyes! And with a quick decision the Devil turned on his heels and leaped through the large living room windows! He disappeared into the ether... taking with him all his little demonic creatures and Spirit Eaters.

"Whew!" I can recall thinking to myself. Finally, I could breathe again.

In what felt to be slow motion, I turned to God and asked, "Why did the Devil come for me?" God replied in a very kind and gentle voice, "He felt your deep despair and vulnerability and believed he could have your Soul".

Instantly, it felt like I not only could hear God's words, but I was also being downloaded with a more comprehensive answer. I was able to see a vision of the Battle for Spirits – not only on the realm here on Earth, but in other galaxies and dimensions as well. I could see how constant negative thoughts and emotions fed negative entities and energies – like those I encountered with the Devil. I realized that our negative thoughts open the doorway to negative entities and energies. And through this vision, I also saw Humanity's largest problem… "Thought Pollution!"

I saw how each word or thought created a wave of energy. I watched as this energy projected out of each person's mind and heart, and then weaved its way into other people's hearts and minds. Eventually this energy became debris and floated out into the cosmos. I saw how we are drowning in this invisible, yet very tangible negative energy.

The message came through that it's time we cleaned up our own garbage! We can turn our entire world around through cleaning up our stinking-thinking thoughts – especially through media such as the internet, radio, television, and what is to come…

There's an old saying, "You are what you eat". I came to see these words also apply to our mental diet as well. The thoughts, words and images we feed ourselves, also show up in our posture, skin tone, brightness in our eyes, energy levels and our all-around demeanor. If we choose to feed ourselves constant negative crap, then we'll soon reflect what we've been putting inside ourselves. Both physically and mentally.

But if we choose to feed ourselves positive words, thoughts, feeling and affirmations, then we'll also reflect our mental diet. We'll shine! And no longer will we be on the radar of these negative energetic parasites… The Vision's Voice then said,

"Goodness will prevail if called upon.
It is the natural rule of order."

The Voice continued, "You need to forgive yourself for all that you have done or said. There is no sense in re-living your 'perceived mistakes' over and over again from the past. You can never go back. The past is the past. Stop looking down and instead bring your chin up my dear" he added. I was having a hard time accepting this idea, so the Voice said, "Consider this,"

'The breath you just expelled is gone, correct?
You can never take it back or breathe it over
again the same way… so let it go.

Move on... and take a new breath!
For each new step, and each new breath brings with it,
New Life and New Possibilities'

Hearing these words, my body instantly reacted in a shower of goosebumps all over my arms and legs... Immediately, the Vision's Voice said, "What you've known as goosebumps, is perhaps better termed as 'truthbumps'... because this reaction is your body's natural communication with self, in hearing a truth (and recognizing its vibration). When your truthbumps rise up, it is an indication for you to be alert to what is being said or shown to you. And when this occurs, no longer dismiss or doubt what is before you - for it is the truth... Your body is showing you so."

Turning back to ask God another question, I discovered he and Jesus had disappeared. They had vanished into thin air! I found myself alone again in my dimly lit studio suite. Thankfully the Devil had disappeared as well. I just stood there for a moment in silence – feeling grateful to be free from the darkness once and for all. I thought to myself, "God's right you know... Today is the first day of the rest of my life! And by golly, today I'm choosing to be (and do) better for myself and others. From this day forward, I'll be a better person!"

In retrospect, this was a wonderful declaration to make, but what I've come to learn over time is that every time you make a bold statement like this, you inevitably are given a chance to apply it. Some say that it's God's way of testing you… but I see it more like it's an opportunity to apply what was just learned and declared.

Well, sure enough, within minutes of making this statement to the Universe, the doors of opportunity opened up wide for me! And I was given the chance to choose a new way of seeing this world. Of learning how to use words and thoughts differently. And I was also shown tools that I could have never dreamed of before. The only thing was – this knowledge didn't come in the nicest of ways. Because soon, I found myself trapped deep inside something. Something that I really didn't know if I'd ever get free from. This 'something' was called the "Black Void".

"The past should only be viewed periodically through the rearview mirror –
as you focus on the road ahead" - CK

CHAPTER 7

NEVER SO GRATEFUL

With God and Jesus gone, I found myself standing in the middle of my living room all by myself. I was looking around my tiny apartment and discovered the hole in the living room floor was gone as well. I looked down at my feet and saw my body was no longer transparent. I was solid!

"I'm ALIVE!" I exclaimed to the empty room! "Hallelujah!"

I was never so grateful for vomit covered clothes in all my life! However, within seconds of standing there, I began to shiver... Hard! With teeth chattering, I walked back over to my bed and stripped off all my clothes. I then pulled the dirty sheets off the bed and threw them into the corner of the room. I jumped under the blankets trying to get warm. Putting my back up against the wall, I decided to try to close my eyes and get some sleep, but my mind was swirling. I couldn't stop trying to piece together everything that had just happened.

As my body began to warm up under the covers, I started to question my sanity. I decided this close call with the Devil was a liquor induced hallucination. "There really is no God" I said to myself. "I must have been really drunk to dream this one up!" Yet questions still lingered... like, "How was it that I was stone cold sober all of a sudden, when I was completely incapacitated just a short time earlier? I fought to grasp for some rational explanation and said to myself, "Maybe this whole scenario did actually happen? Maybe there is a God! Naw... Couldn't be. Could there?" I was so confused. One thing was for sure, I really needed to stop drinking!

I tried everything to sleep! I tossed and turned and finally decided to meditate. But as I laid on my back and looked up at the ceiling, my heart sunk! I nearly screamed out loud in horror! "Oh my God! What the Hell is that???"

Just when I thought I was safe, it was back!

"Where love lives, fear cannot exist" - CK

CHAPTER 8

I AM SAFE

To my horror I saw a dense, black mist, slowly creeping into my apartment from the center of the ceiling again! "Oh my God! The Devil is back!" I thought to myself.

Panicking, I began to say out loud, "Ok yes... There is a God! I believe in God! God is real! God is good! Yes! PLEASE God, just be by my side again! I'm so sorry for doubting you. I believe! I believe! I believe! Can you please come back just one more time and help me keep this darkness away?"

With no response coming from Creator, I decided to quickly jump down onto the floor and pray even harder! "Maybe he didn't hear me" I thought to myself. Getting down on my knees, I began to recite at hyper speed the only two prayers I was taught as a little girl...

The first prayer was a regular bedtime ritual with my Mom that we would do every night before going to sleep. And now over 20 years later, I was once again intertwining my fingers and clutching them together in desperation! I closed my eyes and bowed my head. I spoke quickly and deliberately out loud, as I said this childhood prayer, that never felt more appropriate!

Now I lay me down to sleep,
I pray the Lord my Soul to keep,
If I should die before I wake,
I pray the Lord my Soul to take.
Amen
God Bless my mother, father, sister, brother….

(As a side note – here's a newer, more pleasant version of this prayer…

Now I lay me down to sleep,
I pray the Lord my Soul to keep,
Guide me safely through the night,
Bless me with the morning light.)

So, I finished the prayer and said a list of everyone and everything that I could think of to bless, while simultaneously asking for help! Once I finished this rushed prayer, I looked up at the ceiling to see if the thick black mist had subsided, but it hadn't! It was still there and growing even larger! I then said another prayer that we always recited in school at the start of every day. It was the 'Lord's Prayer'.

Our Father, who art in Heaven,
Hallowed be thy Name.
Thy Kingdom come
Thy will be done on Earth as it is in Heaven.
Give us this day our daily bread. And forgive us our
trespasses,
As we forgive those who trespass against us.
And lead us not into temptation. But deliver us from
evil.
For Thine is the Kingdom, The power, and the glory,
For ever and ever. Amen.

I had said this prayer a thousand times in my youth, but until this very moment I had never really listened to the actual words. As I prayed out loud, I felt the intension of this prayer... I said it with a whole new conviction! Once finished, I looked up yet again and could see the black cloud was still coming closer and closer! I immediately began to ask God to protect me and to always be by my side. I desperately tried to make a deal with him. 'Please keep me safe! Don't let the Devil take my Soul, and I'll do whatever it is you want me to do! I'll quit drinking! I'll be a better person! I promise!"

In truth, I wasn't really expecting a response, but I did look up again one last time – hoping to hear something... Anything, that would stop this black dense smoke from coming to get me! I just wanted to be safe.

To my surprise, Creator did respond... Within seconds of finishing my desperate prayers, a low, deep, BOOMING voice filled the room! It was so loud, it cracked the silence like a whip! I jumped as the Voice said, "You are safe. Now rest."

I looked back up at the ceiling to see where this voice was coming from, and gasped! The HUGE black cloud-like blanket was filling up the entire room and crawling down the walls towards me! Tears began to roll down my cheeks… I thought to myself, "This is it! I'm going to hell!" My mind continued to spin out of control. I could no longer see the windows across the room through the dense, dark fog. The cloud of blackness was now engulfing me…

I slowly got up off my knees and flopped back down on the bed. I decided to surrender to my fate. I simply decided I was done with fighting. I gave up to the blackness and decided to let it swallow me up completely… Which it did.

"Your words and thoughts are your fingerprints on the universe" - CK

CHAPTER 9

THE BLACK VOID

To my surprise, there was nothing evil meeting me in this black cloud of nothingness. There was no sense of doom or gloom. On the contrary, I began to feel safe and loved. It felt like I had been transported up off my bed and was now floating horizontally in an ocean of infinitely dark, warm, loving water. It was so black inside this cloud, that I could no longer see myself. Yet within the blackness, there seemed to be an internal light. A light where I could see things that were shown to me, when needed. It was so black that it was blinding to the eyes, yet illuminating to the Soul.

Once I got over my frantic fear, I questioned myself, "What the heck is this?" To my surprise, the same deep Voice responded again saying, "This is the Black Void". Immediately the words were accompanied by visions. I saw a memory of an Aboriginal Elder who had been teaching me about our culture in the early 1990's. He said, "To find your path, you must release all attachments and begin again. You must call upon Raven to help you. For Raven is the Gatekeeper of the Black

Void, where all illusion begins".

I asked the Voice, "So am I in the same Black Void that my Native Elder spoke of?" As I asked this question, I had the strangest experience. It was like I was in some sort of Sci-fi movie! I watched in amazement as my thoughts and words became physical waves of energy that I could now see and feel. They flowed out of my mind, like ribbons of silky silicon that stretched out endlessly... disappearing deep into the Black Void.

As I watched my 'thought wave' disappear into the black horizon, I saw something coming back towards me from the edges of the horizon... It was another wave that was returning to me at an alarming speed! Somehow, I knew this new wave was bringing back the answers I was looking for. I tensed up, thinking I was going to be hit hard! But instead, the wave washed over (and through) me like a soothing flow of warm, gentle air.

The giant wave felt like a huge dose of love – cleansing me. Then the wave's aftermath spoke in the kindest of voices and said, "Yes, this is the place of reinvention. Where you will start over energetically if you so choose. This is the state where all is infinite with possibilities."

Another wave of energy came over me! This one showed that we can 'reboot' and reinvent ourselves here in the Black Void.

This is where the illusion of life begins, exists and ends all at the same time. It can be entered into at any 'time' we desire, through our own thoughts and wishes.

With the third wave of energy now coming… I understood the Black Void was in fact, 'Time'… Not time as we know it, but in its authentic energetic form. I saw that by giving up and resting completely, I could play with 'Time' and wish it to be whatever I desired. I could get back on my path and 'make up for lost time' so to speak. I could live the life I was meant to live there on Earth. And it all begins in the Black Void with both my new 'projected and protected' thoughts.

Incredibly, I was incapable of having a negative thought in the Back Void! Out of habit, I actually made several attempts to think destructive thoughts. But to my surprise they were stopped in their tracks. Suddenly, I was given the insight of how our thoughts were perhaps our greatest tools! And how they are likely the answer to everything we've been searching for!

Could our thoughts actually be the Holy Grail? Providing us with infinite happiness, abundance, eternal youth and sustenance? I was beginning to think so…

The Voice in the Black Void, (who I believed to be that of the Divine Spirit or Creator) then showed me the magic and power of our thoughts. He demonstrated this through a series of rolling images in my mind. I heard the Voice explain that when we combine a thought with a desire, it sparks or lights up inside of us! Our thoughts then actually project outside of our bodies like a movie. These 'mind movies' display outwardly and can be picked up by everyone else's subconscious and conscious minds. Others can see what we are feeling and thinking. In essence, our thoughts become our calling cards and invitations for others to respond to.

I then saw that this process applies to both positive and negative thoughts. I was shown the example that if you're thinking about finding your perfect job or mate – the more you focus on joy-filled thoughts combined with positive emotions, the faster you'll find your match (otherwise known as your 'corresponding experience'). And the same is equal to that of negative thinking and manifesting drama and trauma in your life. What you think, you attract like a magnet. And what you create in your life all depends on the thought-movie you project outwardly. I realized I was witnessing the mechanics of the Law of Attraction.

We all know by now that if we practice stinkin-thinking thoughts, we'll attract not so pleasant experiences. But if we practice healthy or loving thoughts… we'll attract what we desire!

Walt Whitman once said,

**"The powerful play goes on and you may contribute a verse…
What will your verse be?"**

So, what will your verse or mind-movie be?" The Voice asked me. "What is it that you will focus on from this day forward?"

"Hmm" I thought to myself, "I'm not sure…" I could then see in the Waves of Wisdom that the only way to determine our best and highest outcome is through constantly monitoring our own thoughts. I could see clearly that this was the only tool we need to grow as a global community. The goal is to get to the point that we stop negative thoughts before their seeds begin to grow. This is an internal 'mind-muscle' we all have which needs to be exercised daily through self-regulation, awareness and inspiring thoughts.

The Black Void's "Waves of Wisdom" continued sharing even more down-loads with me. They said, "In the beginning it may be challenging for you to release disempowering thoughts, but over time it will get easier. The best thing to do if a thought catches your attention and feels unkind or harmful in any way, is to ask yourself this simple question…"

"Is this a loving thought?"

"If your thought isn't loving, then throw it into the Cosmic Garbage Can up in the sky! Release the thought and replace it with one that is empowering and positive."

I then saw an image of me having fun playing basketball with my thoughts. I'd crumple up the negative image and toss it into the Cosmic Garbage Can… God would then collect all the debris and transform my negative thoughts into such beauty. I saw myself cheering and giving myself two points! Screaming, "YES! Woo Hoo, I did it!" And I'd danced around celebrating in my mind's eye…

It was clear, I was taking my first steps in letting go of habitual negative thinking. The Voice then said, "The key is to not settle for mediocracy. Keep searching for your best possible thought and then ask yourself,

"Is this the best possible thought I can think of right now?"

If it isn't, then repeat the previous steps over and over again until you can answer, "Yes! This thought feels REALLY good!"

He continued, "This cycle of 'bettering your thoughts' can go on until you find yourself vibrating with excitement! Soon you'll have such confidence and you'll be filled with images of infinite possibilities!"

"It's incredible" I thought to myself! "All this by simply asking two simple questions and then following through until the feeling inside is elevated! Wow!"

Suddenly a huge banner popped up in my mind! It was floating in front of me and read…

"Many are called, but few are chosen"

The deep Voice interrupted the silence and asked, "Do you recognize these words? I told him that I did. He said, "The purer intention of this statement is this…

"All are called upon, but few choose to answer"

I saw clearly that most people don't know how to answer their calling or live their life's purpose… That was when the Voice in the Black Void spoke again and said, "Each Soul is called upon. Each Spirit has a purpose-filled life. The choice is theirs whether they'll step up and accept their destiny, or choose instead to be fear-filled and live a life of mediocracy."

There was a long pause and then the Voice continued… "If for instance, you choose to answer your own calling. The way to do so, is to choose to live in a higher frequency of empowering and uplifting thoughts on a regular basis. You'll need to connect often through silence, and consistently grow your internal light. Soon you'll look back and will struggle to remember the last time you had a self-destructive conversation with yourself. This is the mind-set that will be needed in order for you to achieve your calling. You'll need to become your own greatest ally, release self-doubt and anger, and be open to what is possible!" the Voice said.

This idea then led to the next lesson while floating in the Black Void… "How to Master the Law of Attraction like never before!"

CHAPTER 10

LAW OF ATTRACTION

To further illustrate the power of the Law of Attraction and
how to use the tools of positive imaging - the Voice in the
Black Void revealed to me the next lesson. It came by way of
a memory...

I was shown the memory of my fiancé Michael and my first
date. We were walking around the Seawall in Vancouver's
Stanley Park. I could see that because we were sharing such a
deep connection and sense of love for one another already, our
minds and hearts were beginning to open up on a whole new
level! We strolled along and chatted about our lives and what
we had experienced so far. But there was also a lot of time
where we both just walked in silence... Appreciating the sunset
and all its beauty. Now looking back, I can see that we were
both truly living in the moment of the 'Now'.

I remember we were both silent and feeling such gratitude for meeting one another, when suddenly I saw a beam of light slowly begin to shine out of Michael's forehead! It appeared as a projection that lit up and stretched out about two feet in front of him. I was stunned! "What the hell is that?" I thought to myself! I didn't say anything because I didn't want to interrupt it. It felt organic and grew the more I trusted that it was something special to witness. I really wanted to see what the heck this projection would do!

Looking into it, I had an understanding that it was called a 'thought-movie' or 'mind-movie' and that I was seeing Michael's thoughts. It was WILD! I could see Michael's thoughts and hear his words before he even spoke them! He was thinking, "someday, we will all be one". Well, this was such a random thought – especially for 1993! Michael still hadn't said anything out loud to me. He was enjoying the sunset. His mind however was spinning and I could see its every movement.

Mike then turned towards the ocean and said in a contemplative voice, "I believe that…" I interrupted his words and said, "Yes, I know… I agree." He stopped and laughed saying, "Wow! What did you think I was going to say? Because it has nothing to do with what we were just talking about a few minutes ago." I laughed nervously and said, "You were going to say that one day we will all be one. Living together as one healthy, loving, respectful and supportive community – despite our differences…"

Well, Michael just stood there stunned! He finally asked in a slow and cautious voice, "How the heck did you know that was what I was going to say? I mean, it's not like it had anything to do with what we were talking about?" He added, "This was so off the cuff… and no one says shit like this! At least, no one I know of."

I hesitated and then decided to be totally open, even at the risk of losing him. I said, "It was the strangest thing ever. I've never seen anything like it before… I could see your thoughts as they were projecting out of your 3rd eye in front of you! It looked like something you'd see in an old, smoke-filled movie theatre. You know… The see-through beam of light that goes from the projector to the screen. Only this was your thoughts I was seeing in the cone-shaped projection."

Michael was silent. I tried to reassure him that this could be a natural thing that we're all capable of seeing and having. I said to him, "I think I saw it because we are being so honest and open with one another. I believe it's a new level of communication perhaps." I then added, "When you think of it, they say we only use 5% of our brains… well, maybe through complete honesty and openness, we can tap into greater abilities? Maybe by being completely honest and vulnerable with one another, we're opening up to the ability of being telepathic or something like that. It makes sense, right?"

I continued, "I think secrets create walls between people. And you and I Michael seems to have no walls because we have no secrets! I think we're opening up to what is possible."

Michael was digesting the idea and slowly nodding his head as he agreed. He was still stunned… trying to take it all in. We began to walk again in silence. But I did notice his mind-movie was shut down now. I was worried that I might have scared him off. All of a sudden, I was REALLY wishing I could see his thoughts again.

Suddenly, almost like I was on a bungy cord, I was pulled backwards out of this memory of our first date and landed back in the Black Void. The Voice told me I was about to be shown the 'mechanics of how our thoughts work'. And with that, I was pushed forward rather aggressively and flew through – what I now know to be a wormhole…

I landed back in the same memory of our first date. Only this time I was being given a full step-by-step explanation of how Michael's thoughts worked from a more biological and physiological view-point.

Immediately, I saw Mike's body standing in front of me, but everything had become frozen in time. Mike's body was now semi-transparent. It was as if he was standing in front of an advanced X-Ray machine. I could see beyond his skeletal system… I could see all his muscles, circulatory system and his nervous system as well! I was guided visually while the Voice explained each step of how the 'Power of Thought' works.

I was shown that when Michael mixed a thought with his feelings in the heart area, it ignited a spark of energy! Almost instantly, this spark traveled up through his chakras or energy column. It woke up his entire neurological system through the spine. I could see sparks of energy firing off inside of Mike – like a chain reaction going off. The nerve cells were coming alive and were responding to Mike's initial thoughts. More so... they were reacting to the way he felt about his thoughts!

The sparks of light continued to travel up his spine and then stopped in the center of Michael's brain. It ignited yet again with another flash of light! Right in the center of his pineal gland. Instantly, his thoughts were projected forward, zooming out through his third eye in the middle of his forehead - like rocket ships of desire! (As Abraham Hicks would say)

I could then see inside the cone shaped projection. There were a series of thin red, green and blue filaments which began to appear. These streams of zig-zagging energies reached out beyond the projection. They began to dart off, disappearing into the air in front of us. But I also saw they were like homing pigeons. These filaments would return to Michael in time, but for now they seemed to have a mission. They appeared to be searching like a magnet for a corresponding person, place or experience to Michael's thoughts. It reminded me of a nerve synapse, searching to connect with another nerve cell.

Again, I was jerked out of this memory and travelled back into the Black Void. The ever-present Voice was now telling me that both positive and negative thoughts take this same energetic pathway through the body. Both thought vibrations ignite the same way. What was so intriguing though, was here in the Black Void negative thoughts couldn't project or come alive at all! They couldn't even leave my mind! Heck… They couldn't spark, grow or blossom. It was like a gatekeeper was keeping all the negative thoughts at bay. Only thoughts that were in (or of) the highest concern could be seen, felt, or manifested here in the Black Void.

My next thought was, "How do I create this level of positive imaging in my daily life outside of the Black Void?" The answer came in a series of questions that I heard myself asking…

- First, are we ever outside of the Black Void?

- Is the Black Void an illusion? And if so, then where are our Spirits and Souls in all of this?

- And are they one-in-the-same, or are our Spirits and Souls different entities?

With these question – came the next set of Lessons…

CHAPTER 11

SPIRIT - VS - SOUL

While floating in the Black Void, I asked a question that I had thought about for a very long time, but never heard an answer that rang true for me. I asked the Divine Voice, "What is the difference between a Soul and Spirit?" The Waves of Wisdom washed over me again and I heard these words and felt this explanation.

Simply put, I saw the Soul is what we call our 'Higher Self'. It remains with Creator in the collective ocean of what we call Heaven. I then heard...

'Spirit is an extension of the Soul'

I could see the explanation. It showed that the Spirit is assigned to a 'Body' on Earth, and they agree to grow together. Like a tree and its roots. So, it's not surprising that the Old English word for 'body' is 'trunk'.

I was told, "The Spirit is the Body's life-force or battery". I then saw when the Soul enters into a Soul Contract to experience Earth for example, tether-lines are attached between the Spirit (below) and the Soul (above). It looked a bit like a marionette. The difference is, the Spirit has a mind of itself (its self) and isn't totally dependent upon the Soul to make decisions. They work together. The tether-line was more of an energetic 'Soul Connection' than anything else. The strings looked like a telephone line that was used for communication. But I could also see that this line between the Spirit and Soul was so much more! It was similar to the life cord an astronaut has – connecting them to the space station when they venture outside of the craft. The line allows for safety, communication, oxygen, and provides a life-force – keeping the astronaut alive. Well, the same is true for the Soul Connection. Because without this energetic tether-line, the Spirit, Soul, Body and Mind would all cease to function as a unit.

Looking deeper, I could see in the explanation that another tether-cord also exists between the Spirit and Body as well... That's when it hit me! These tether lines also contain our Streams of Consciousness! Where our Minds are rooted from. These lines were silver in color... This would explain why so many people have seen a 'silver cord' linking their Spirit to their physical bodies during astral projections or out-of-body experiences.

I asked through my thoughts, "So how do we see the Silver Cord from a distance while having an out-of-body-experience (OBE) if our Minds are held within this Stream of Consciousness?" The Voice quickly replied, "You're thinking from a linear viewpoint. The Mind is connected to not only the filaments and energy of the cord, but to all matter! From your cells to the infinite! Your Mind can travel wherever it desires. Freely! And in time you will discover your body can travel with it."

I then saw an image that showed me, our memories are not 'stored' in our brains… They float outside of ourselves in our force fields and surrounding ether. They are called upon like a reverse action of the projections of our thoughts. They are sucked and absorbed into our cells, where they travel to all parts of the body. Hence why we call it 'cellular memory'.

I thought to myself, "This would also explain why we feel so deeply connected to the Universe when we meditate regularly. This is because by praying or stilling our minds, we're strengthening our tether-lines and Soul Connections – thereby making our energy field and roots even stronger!" It seemed to me, we're just one giant plant! We have a life-force that runs through our roots, trunk and branches, and eventually we all bear fruit… (one way or another)

With this understanding, I could see how one person could make a huge difference in the world without ever being aware of it! We're all connected after all through these filaments of energy. And our roots touch one another – just like the trees. What you think and feel affects me, and what I think and feel affects you. Through implementing consistently positive thoughts – together, we could clean up the stinkin-thinking thought pollution and change the world as we know it.

This insight filled me with such hope! I relaxed even more into the Black Void. I decided that if I ever got out of this place and returned to the life I knew back on Earth; I'd trust in the process of co-creating all that is desired! "It's easy", I thought to myself. "It really is just that easy to think our way into living a heavenly life on Earth."

The lessons seemed to finish, and I was left to float in utter darkness. The black waves of wisdom calmed down and everything was still. I called out to the Voice, but there was no response. Weirdly enough, my own voice in the Void had changed. It no longer had that deep, rich tone. My voice was now sounding tinny and hollow, and I realized I was alone. All the magic I had been surrounded by seemed to settle down and was having a rest.

That was when the last lesson began to bubble up in me. I felt trapped and completely blind in the utter darkness once again. I didn´t know what to do next and began to feel a bit claustrophobic… It took everything in me not to panic!

Looking back, the sensation was similar to being in a cave or a float tank that was void of light. I didn't know where was up or down. I felt invisible. The only thing present in this vastness was my mind…

So instead of panicking, I decided to 'closed my eyes' as such, and trust in this place enough to fall asleep. There was nowhere else to go after all… I could either struggle and panic, or I could succumb to the overwhelming feeling of love that was ever-present. I chose to trust and soon drifted off into the deepest of sleeps. And when I woke up… it was daylight!

Miraculously, I found myself out of the Black Void… I was laying on my bed again in my tiny studio suite in downtown Vancouver. I felt renewed and refreshed! Wow!!! I had a new lease on life! I could start all over again and be a better person. I vowed to be free of alcohol, disempowering thoughts and to be kinder to myself and others.

Deciding to start the day, I got up and thought to myself, 'I'd likely never hear from God again'… but what came next was truly extraordinary! I came to understand that we are never alone… Creator is always with us. In all ways.

"If you're always trying to be normal, you will never know how amazing you can be"
By Maya Angelou

CHAPTER 12

THE HIPPY DIPPY HOUSE

After dying the first time, I was surprised to wake up the next morning with many unexpected gifts… I soon discovered I was able to hear, see and feel things that others couldn't, on a whole new level! I always had 'gifts' growing up, but this was different! I now had the ability to throw energy if I was tired or mad. I could burn out light bulbs, fry microwaves, blow car engines, and flatten tires (without even touching the cars). But I had to be furious to do this. I also became very good at protecting loved ones and myself with white lights of energy and positive thoughts. I had returned with new abilities – many I'm still discovering to this day.

The first clue that something had changed within me came when I woke up after fighting with the Devil and experiencing the Black Void. I woke up feeling refreshed. Got up and crossed the living room floor to go to the bathroom. While doing so, I looked up at the ceiling and asked jokingly, "Are you still there?" Suddenly, a younger man's voice kindly whispered in my right ear, "Go to the front door. There, you'll find a gift." Well, I just about jumped out of my own skin! I quickly spun around because it sounded like he was right beside me... But no one was there.

Deciding to trust this new Voice, I went over and opened my door to the hallway of the apartment building. There I found a newspaper placed neatly on my door mat. I burst out laughing because I NEVER bought newspapers! Growing up I couldn't read very well (if at all) so why would I have a newspaper? I then heard this same male Voice say, "Look at the classified section."

I opened up the one-inch-thick Saturday Newspaper to the exact page of the housing classifieds. There in BOLD print was an ad for my future home – my beloved hippy dippy house! Within an hour of seeing this ad, I had cleaned up and zoomed across the city to go see this large West-Coast styled, 3-story estate. It had many bedrooms available for rent. Most were shared rooms at $175/bed, but only one bedroom was private. It was expensive back then at $250/month. Within ten minutes, I had signed the rental agreement on the spot for the quaint private bedroom. It was separate from all the other bedrooms in the house, and was on the second floor just off the kitchen and sitting area... I simply loved it!

I drove back to my downtown suite and met with Carmen, the

apartment manager. Miraculously, he let me move out without any penalties! My best girlfriend at the time, Laura Plathan also lived in the building one floor below me. We were inseparable and the only two single girls who lived there at the time. Carmen was a sweet older man who was a heavy drinker. We'd flirt with him all the time in the elevator or front entrance, and it'd brighten up all of our days. We were always laughing with him and having such fun! So, when it came time to move out without any notice, there was no problem. Carmen loved the two of us and was flexible. In fact, Laura and he even helped me drag my old mattress downstairs, and we put it in the dumpster in the back alley.

I cleaned up my tiny suite and by 7 pm that night, I was moved into my new quaint room in the Hippy House. Luckily, my new room had every bit of furniture I needed. It had a built-in bed and mattress, a stone fireplace, a built-in desk and closet, with a HUGE window that looked out into the garden and over-looked the hot tub and outdoor shower area. It was lovely!

My new communal home was a vegetarian, non-smoking, non-drinking place, which had 11 to 22 roommates in it. The amount of people in the main house depended on the workshops that were being offered in the secondary house in the back of the property.

The first night I arrived, I lit the fireplace in my new bedroom and began the practice of writing in my journal. I didn't want to ever forget these amazing experiences that I was blessed to have - especially during the next year that I'd be in this extraordinary house...

This communal home was one of those unique places you hear about where gifted artists, writers and visionaries would gather – like the Group of 7. The house became a magnet for brilliant minds. People would just show up, like Eckhart Tolle and Eric Edmeades... They would come over and join us around the table for great vegetarian food and even better debates and discussions. We were all kids back then. In our early and late 20's. Long before anyone was ever published or had become famous. The conversations we'd have often ended up being the stuff that future books and lectures were made of. In fact, Quantum Physics and Nanotechnology were just starting to be openly discussed in small groups, and we (at the Hippy House) were one of those groups. The idea of taking the 'Red Pill' wouldn't come along for another 6 years yet!

It had felt like I was reliving these events all over again, when suddenly I remembered this was only a memory! Suddenly, I found myself standing in front of the Council of Men in the White Void, yet again. And I began to remember the last question I was asked by the Elder before I went back in time.... He asked, "Do you remember when you called out to us for help?" I was surprised at how many memories I had relived since that question was asked. And now I found myself filled with questions that I needed to be answered as well...

"The living soul of man, once conscious of its power, cannot be quelled"
By Horace Mann

CHAPTER 13

THE RISK OF EARTH

I found myself back in the White Void again. Sitting in front of God and the Council of Men. Only this time, I was asking them a question. I wanted to know why I died again…

I asked them all, "Why after listening to the 7-foot Angel, and turning my life around, am I now sitting in front of you and being judged? I did everything that was asked of me and yet here I am! Dead! And for the second time! Why???"

The radiant Council Member reassured me that I wasn't being judged. He said I was brought to the White Void because I was still judging myself far too much and needed to forgive myself. He said that they 'brought me here' to help me in this process. So, I could be strong enough to complete my mission.

"Mission" I laughed out loud! "What mission could I have? I was a wounded, drunk, bartender back home! What mission could I do that would be so vital?" I looked down at my feet, shaking my head in disbelief. The Elder firmly said while hearing my thoughts, "This is precisely why you are here. Let us look at how special and unique you are. In fact, let us look at how brilliant each and every Soul is, and how they come to choose their own missions shall we?"

I shrugged and agreed to listen some more...

The Chair of the Council of Men began to explain, "Before going to Earth or elsewhere, Souls can choose from an infinite array of directions and experiences to learn and grow from. There are many experiences to choose from. Many of you have chosen Earth for your place of growth. This is because Earth has a very unique composition. It is one of a few options in which you can decide your fate completely, through the state of 'Free Will'.

I could see images begin to appear again that accompanied the Council Member's words. I saw that we all have agreed to be part of this endless loop experiment. Collectively, we have a greater mission and this is to move beyond the energetic loop. I was shown that the only way to stop the endless cycle and to progress forward, is to consistently practice love for one another; for all other living and non-living things; and for ourselves as well. I saw an image of a time in our future where humans will love everything from insects to animals! From one another to even our so-called enemies. Wars are in the past. We must practice love! It all starts from within each and every one of us. The more of us who live and breathe love – the more loving our environment will be!

This insight reminded me of the fable of the 100th Monkey by Ken Keyes, back in 1981. The lesson of the book was basically, 'Once one of us starts to learn a new way of living or thinking – we can all benefit from it! Collectively we can create an evolved, loving civilization that is free of war and conflict. It just starts with one person deciding to break the mold and live a different way'.

The Council then showed me a series of fairytales in my mind. (Which I thought was odd at first) Many of the fairytales had the same message – that love conquers all! Love wakes up the dead and sleeping beauties! It melts even the iciest of hearts! It can bring back life to flowers, trees, and all living things! A loving kiss can be magical! It can heal pain instantly... It heals all wounds! (Every parent knows this after all, when they kiss their injured child better).

The images in my mind began to expand. I could soon see through the constant practice of love, our outcome here on Earth could have an everlasting effect on the whole Universe and beyond! I saw how our choices effect fellow Souls in other dimensions and Galaxies as well! Souls who we would call 'Aliens' or 'ETs' here on Earth – but were in fact Souls who live in places that we could have chosen to go to instead of coming to 'Earth'. I saw how all these 'Alien Nations' are also connected to the God Source Energy.

We may look different and act different, but in the end... we're all pieces to the same greater puzzle.

The Elder Member went on to say, "The unique thing about choosing to come to Earth rather than any other plane, is that with Earth you are constantly growing in one way or another. You enter this dimension of Earth at great risk, because you can either grow and advance your Spirit and Soul in a loving and empowered direction, or..." he said with a pause, "You can do the opposite and return worse-off than whence you came".

I could see that the Elder chose his words carefully here. Because while he was talking, I thought to myself, "Oh ya... We could destroy our Spirit with our choices on Earth." The Elder heard this thought and quickly corrected me. (while still simultaneously having the other conversation). He said to my mind, "You cannot 'destroy' your Spirit. It is pure energy. But you can transform or transmute your Spirit and Soul into another form of a lower vibration. Hence why we say, 'You could return worse off than whence you came'.

This is why Earth comes at a great risk. You can deplete your Soul's vitality, as much as you can grow it beyond measure. It truly is your choice of the life you live.

I thought about the person I was back on Earth, and how I had been dying inside for such a long time with depression. I wasn't the same beautiful, optimistic, little sprite I had been as a child, or even as a young woman. My Spirit had disintegrated from its former self, and my heart was heavy with guilt, sadness and even anger on a regular basis.

I looked at the Elder and with an open heart said to him, "Yes, I do fully understand that my future is mine to create. I need to have healthier thoughts and a greater desire to live a joyful life." He nodded in agreement. The Elder then said, "We were very concerned with your plight. To go to the depths you did, was notable. Some never make it back. They spin or hide in the endless loop of despair." He sat silently looking at me for what seemed to be a long period of time. I broke the silence by saying, "I do understand. Thank you".

The entire Council sat there quietly just looking at me… Then the Elder's face shifted. He gave me the brightest smile and added, "But we are very pleased to say that you have learned so much… We have summoned you here today out of celebration because we want to offer you praise on your transformation! We acknowledge the strength and faith it took for you to call for help and to turn your life's path around. We are so very pleased with your growth and choices made. We want to share with you that you are loved and cherished. You have not only healed your mind but your heart as well…

You have listened and followed through with uplifting thoughts and actions, and as a result, your Soul has grown so much! Well done."

A deep sense of relief washed over my body, as I let out a huge sigh… I realized I had been holding my breath all this time. I said to the Council while breaking down into tears, "I thought you brought me here to punish me! To send me back to the dark side. Or to tell me to stay away from Michael because he is so innocent and good, and I've done things that are, well… They were terrible quite frankly."

God then spoke with such warmth, "You are more than worthy of Michael's love. In fact, you are so loved that we've brought you here! We'd like to share with you a glimpse of your life from not only our perspective, but everyone else's. We want you to see the love you are surrounded with. This is one of our greatest gifts for you… Your life's review".

With these words and another wave of God's hands, a 9-inch round, brilliant, golden white sphere materialized and began to float in between us! God then said, "Through this hologram, you will be able to see, feel and know the past, present and future of your timeline. Images and sensations will fill you in all ways! It will be as if you are living all of these experiences over again with great clarity and speed." Creator then added while gesturing to the hologram, "It is time that we showed you something that will help greatly in your healing. Let us begin…

"Don't judge a man until you've walked two moons in his moccasins"
Native American Indian Proverb

CHAPTER 14

9-D HOLOGRAM

I felt nervous of what was to come while staring into this 9-dimensional hologram. (Don't ask me what a 9D Hologram is because I don't have a clue. I was just told its name as it hovered and spun in a constant rhythm between us. I was also told there is a 12D Hologram and its meaning will also be revealed in our lifetime back on Earth). I had never heard of sacred geometry before, (it was 1993 after all) but I suspect this is what I was witnessing.

The hologram itself was a huge circle and within it was a large cube filling the sphere completely! (I sketched a diagram of it on the following page) Within the cube were four large pyramids, that also filled up the cube completely. And in the very center where all four pyramids came together at the tip, there was a magnificent speck of light. It seemed to be alive! A

living, breathing, conscious tool... And by simply looking at this tiny bright yellow light in the center, I felt drawn into it – like a vacuum sucking me up into a wormhole! But I resisted the pulling sensation of the hologram. I was afraid to go into it and see what was on the other side. "What if I get stuck in there forever?" I thought to myself. But God gently reassured me, "This is our gift to you. This is your life's review. We want you to see your life from our perspective and from all those around you. You are safe.

I took a deep breath and relaxed. I decided to look deep into the light at the center of the hologram. It immediately came closer to me. I could see that the light had a very tiny movie playing inside it. I could actually begin to see people's faces! And with that thought, instantly I was sucked up and disappeared deep into the hologram... It felt like I was zooming down a brilliant-colored circular slide. It felt like I was flying out of control! Suddenly, I came to a stop and found myself in an empty black space. "I'm back in the Black Void again!" I chuckled to myself... "Woo Hoo!" And sure enough, from a distance I could feel those same familiar waves of energy heading my way. "Oh boy! Here we go again!" I said with excitement!

This time there were many waves coming at me at high speed!

Then suddenly the waves divided and became two huge 8-foot-tall columns! These black walls of water were still heading towards me. I felt a bit like Moses, and how he must have felt – standing on the floor of the ocean with the sea dividing on both sides. I closed my eyes waiting for the waves to hit me once again, but I only felt a rush of air blow past me. I opened my eyes and saw that I was standing in the center of a double-sided Timeline. Images from my past were zooming by me at lightning speed on both sides! It was like I was a sponge soaking up every bit of information possible!

The first image I saw of myself was pre-birth… I could see that I liked to float around outside of my Mom's womb before I was born – observing and getting to know her and the family really well. This was such a joyful time for me. Anticipation! And there was so much love around all of us. I was feeling really happy to be born.

I popped my head out of this memory and continued to stand with both feet planted. The rush of the timeline on both sides was nearly knocking me over! I randomly decided to look to my right and instantly I was seeing the first day I was brought home from the hospital. My brother Tom and sister Cathy saw me for the first time and weren't so impressed. I was born quite ill and had sores and scabs all over my body. Both of them said to our Mom, "Oh my God! She's ugly!" I could sense that my sister had been quite excited at the thought of having a baby sister. She thought she'd have someone to play with. But because I was so sickly and cried so much, I could see that I felt more of a nuisance to my siblings than anything else.

I remembered feeling all my life that Cathy had resented me for taking our Mom away from her so much. But through this hologram, I saw life from my sister's perspective... I felt her compassion and love, yet also understood how sad she was that our Mom's time was strained in caring for me. I sensed Cathy had felt abandoned. And I could see and feel all our interactions from childhood right up to the present. It was like I was in her head and heart at the same time. I could feel and know my sister's decisions and why she made them. I could see every conversation we had from her perspective – and I finally understood her side of our story together. I saw that she had sacrificed a lot for me, since I was a baby. She did things for me that I had no idea she had done! She had been kind even when I wasn't. And through it all, I felt a great love for her. I saw my sister in a brand-new light...

I thought of my Dad, and instantly I flew out of the memory with my sister and landed in the summary of my Dad's life! I could feel why he chose to be a boxer after being beaten so badly as a child by his own father. I had never met my Grandfather. Didn't even know he existed until I was in my 20's. I saw in this timeline, where my dad and his father's rage came from; and why my Dad decided to pretend his father was dead for most of his life.

My Grandfather had wanted to study medicine, but during WW1 the Govt' discovered he was a skilled marksman and was incredibly talented at throwing weapons and knives. So, Granddad became a sniper during the war, and eventually returned home with a plate in his head from a shrapnel wound.

A few years after his return, Grandad's young wife (my Grandmother) died at the age of 32 from a heart attack. Granddad was not able to cope or care for their 3 small children by himself – so one day he just got up and left! The 2 older kids, George (7) and Muriel (13) went to school that fateful day… and Dad being the youngest at age 3, was brought to the neighbors while his Father went to 'work'. My Grandfather never came back for his kids. He simply disappeared.

The neighbor couldn't keep my dad or his siblings, so the boys were placed in an East-side Vancouver Orphanage, and Muriel was sent off to a Convent. It was 1928, and the Orphanage was filthy! There was very little food for the children. But what was abundant? Was a whole lot of abuse… Two years later, the officials found my Grandfather and forced him to take back his kids. By now Granddad had remarried and started another family.

Through the Hologram's Timeline, I could see in my grandfather's heart that he didn't want his previous kids or the memory of his former wife (my Grandmother). I could see his deep sorrow of losing his first wife. She was the love of his life! And I could also feel the intense pain from his head injuries – especially when the kids were screaming and playing. The pain was literally driving him insane!

I then witnessed a key moment between my father and his dad while in the Hologram. Dad was 5-years-old and was sent out to the woodshed to get some wood for the stove. He was so excited to be trusted with this new job. My dad got to the woodpile and asked his father who was sitting on the porch whittling some wood, "Is it this one you want Dad?" My Grandfather who looked to be in his late 20's or early 30's at the time just growled at his son and said, "It's to your right!" I could see my dad hesitate. He was just a little boy still and no one had taught him in the Orphanage which was his right or left. So, I watched as my young father made the decision to take another small step to his side. He was praying he was stepping in the right direction. Dad gingerly asked his father again, "Is it... this one?" Suddenly, my Grandfather stood up and yelled with such rage! "NO! THIS IS THE ONE I WANT!" Just then Granddad threw the carving knife that was in his hand and sent it flying through the air towards his own son's head! The knife whizzed past my father's tiny face and twanged as it buried itself deep into the log beside my father's trembling little body... My Dad of course tried so hard to hold back his tears, because he knew another beating would be coming if he cried. It was in this moment I witnessed the level of abuse my father had grown up with. It was amazing to me that he turned out to be the generous Soul he did. He could have been a monster, but instead he gave so much of his life to charity and helping others through his work as a physical therapist. Dad was later inducted into the Sports Hall of Fame for his years in Sports Medicine – with both professional and amateur athletes. He touched so many Souls with his encouragement and wisdom.

Moving past my Father's life-review, I quickly saw my Mom's memories of her life. I watched as she first met my Dad. I saw and heard her inner dialogue as she decided that he was the one for her! She too had a similar calling card as my Dad regarding abuse as a child.

Mom was Native (better known as an Indian in those days) and was separated from her Mother and brother as she was placed in a residential school at the age of three. Mom was also abused by the priests and nuns but never spoke of it – ever! It wasn't until after her death that I learned the truth of my Mother's upbringing from her best friend. I have the greatest admiration for our Mom because despite all the abuse she experienced, she decided early on that her past did not equal her future. She chose to live differently that her upbringing. I dare say that my Mom rewrote her past and lived life as if she had only known love throughout her entire life… And what a beautiful Soul she was as a result!

Next, I travelled further down the timeline and peeked into another significant event in my life… It was the moment I met my ex-boyfriend in the Polo Ralph Lauren shop – where he worked. I was shopping for some clothes and looked up and there he was! The timeline skipped forward 2 years to a discussion we were having with his dad about our surprise pregnancy. I could feel his father's heart at the time of our abortion. I saw why he was so angry. I also saw the reasons behind the timing of his mother's death. Her funeral was the same day and time as our abortion. None of his family knew where I was… or what I was doing. I could see and feel the concern from his siblings for my sudden disappearance on the day of their mother's funeral. I saw my ex's sister asking him,

"Where's Carrie?" My ex stuttered and made up an excuse for me. His sister wasn't buying it… She was a smart cookie and knew something was up.

I watched in the timeline as they lowered my ex's mother into the ground with all his family gathered around. The sadness was overwhelming. Suddenly, I found the hologram took me sharply to the right! I was now flying at high speed across the city towards the hospital where I was having the abortion. I flew through the walls of the building and immediately found my 24-year-old self being transferred onto a gurney. I watched myself wipe away my tears as I was about to be brought in for surgery. Soon I was being wheeled down the hallway towards the operating room by the most aggressive nurse ever! She was violently ramming the gurney into the swinging doors and walls, while telling me 'I was a Sinner'! The nurse and I came flying around the corner with the gurney on two wheels as we entered into the cold, sterile operating room. She was still quoting biblical scriptures to me with such distain! I watched as she quickly prepped the needle to put me under. She was spitting mad! I finally interrupted her rampage and demanded, "That's enough! I don't want to do this anymore!" I spat back at her. And as I tried to get up and off the gurney, she shoved my head back and quickly rammed the needle into my arm! She told me to shut up and then barked at me - asking for my weight. Once I answered, she realized that she was giving me too much anesthetic for my size, and the last words I heard her say to me were, "Ah Fuck!"

Through this hologram, I began to travel into the Nurse's

timeline. Immediately I saw from her perspective that she had lost a child and much of her family. She was disgusted at the thought of performing an abortion! It was against her faith… Plus, it was May 1988 in British Columbia Canada, and the Premier of the Province had just announced the night before on television, that he'd have to comply with the Supreme Court of Canada´s Order and allow abortions to be performed in BC again – starting first thing in the morning. So here I was… admitted the night before and by 8 am, I was one of the first patients to be having an abortion in the province.

I could see this Nurse was repulsed that I would toss away something she longed for… family! Then I saw and felt the Nurse's fear of losing her job after quoting the Bible to me so much and calling me a 'Sinner'. She knew she overstepped her legal boundaries and could lose her job if I was to complain or tell anyone. So the Nurse made a quick decision to drug me and get it over with. I was given a glimpse into her guilt and the anger she felt while doing the abortion. It would be with her for decades to come.

As it turned out, the timeline showed me that the abortion was the beginning of both of our destruction and ultimate healing. There was no accident this Nurse and my path crossed… even if it was such a violent encounter at the time. I could see how we had a Soul Contract to participate together. I remember praying that hopefully in the end, we'd both choose to heal and grow from this experience.

The big message I got from the 9D Hologram was that when you walk in another's shoes, you receive a different perspective. Zooming through my life was a whirlwind of emotions, where I felt happy, sad, compassionate and challenged all at once! I saw that each person, place and thing I encountered in my lifetime left behind a footprint of profound knowledge and clarity. I now understood that we are never alone on this trip... Because we're an extension of God – just like the Sprit is connected to the Soul. We are all one with Creator. Therefore, we all have the same tether-line connecting us with God-Source Energy - and each other.

At the end of the 'Life-Review' I immediately came flying out of the hologram at great speed! I hit the cloud-like chair so hard that I bounced off of it a couple of times before settling back down. Gaining my composure and getting settled in, I thought to myself, "Wow, that was a rough landing!" God sat in silence with a slight smile of amusement on his face. He was waiting for me to digest what I had just experienced.

I finally broke the silence and said, "Wow... What I've learned is that I didn't have much gratitude in my life. I spent so much time focusing on all the bad stuff that I had done and said to others. There was little room for gratefulness. Plus, I used to use the blame game against other people a lot! For all the rotten things they had said and done to me. What I see now, is they had their own reasons for saying or doing what they did. But these reasons were invisible to me at the time... Probably because I wasn't being compassionate or practicing gratitude for them – or myself for that matter.

I added a final thought and said, "I failed to see all the beauty around me and the goodness that was in my life. I now understand that when I do focus on the love I have for myself and other, everything seems to smooth over and come together more easily. I see now that love, faith and gratitude are the key."

Creator nodded in agreement and gave me the warmest smile. I could see he was pleased that I finally came to love myself unconditionally. I finally received the message that focusing on gratitude was imperative for our Spirit's expansion.

God then said, "Yes, and we are grateful for you as well. We are grateful you never tried to end your life and instead held on… because that would have altered matters. God continued, "We are grateful you instead chose to call and ask for help."

He added, "The giving up on one's gift of life prematurely is something we will talk about next."

CHAPTER 15

SUICIDE

THE REPEAT BUTTON

I had considered suicide so many times in my life... I thought about it for the first time when I was a young girl who was bullied and alienated by virtually every kid in school. Then came relentless thoughts of taking my life after the abortion; and finally, the third bout came after a huge lose and feeling utterly broken, betrayed and distraught.

God and the Elders again nodded as they witnessed my sorrow-filled memories scrolling across my mind. I was back sitting with them in the White Void and the Elder of the Council of Men interrupted my doom and gloom thoughts, and said, "We are so happy that you did not choose to end your life experience early. If you had, you would have entered into an endless loop – which could greatly complicate the life you've chosen to experience on Earth. I wondered what he meant by this and then I began to also wonder, "What would have happened if I had committed suicide?" Instantly the answers began to flow…

I was shown a series of images of what happens when a Spirit chooses suicide. This shook me so much so, that never again could I *ever* consider ending my own life!

I was shown that there are two routes a Suicide Soul takes. One is the easier route – straight to Heaven. Where the Spirit reviews their life, rests a bit, and then returns to start the exact same experience all over again.

The second route was much harder… The torment that the Spirit and Soul takes in this route is far greater than any pain they could have experienced on Earth! This to me was a living Hell! Especially if the Spirit decides to stay trapped for a long period of time, in what looked to be a nightmarish abyss. It can be such a difficult journey if the Spirit chooses to go deeper and deeper into despair – rather than looking for the Light. But it doesn't have to be this way, is what I was shown.

The second, more difficult route looked to be a bleak abyss that was filled with tormented souls. They had lost all hope. It was like a no-man's land, where lost spirits just floated and floundered in a grey, soupy wasteland. I could hear screeching noises and howls of agony in this abyss! And I saw a glimpse every once in a while, of a grotesque face that would pop up and out of the thick mist surrounding the lost souls! I saw how it immediately jarred these suicide souls and sent them into an even deeper depression. It was horrible to watch... It was obvious this was all self-induced. These Spirits were suspended in an in-between state because they had lost the connection between their Spirit and Soul. They had given up and lost all hope, faith and gratitude in life.

The good news is, the Suicidal Soul could change all of this around instantly, because the Light Beings were never really far away. All these Souls had to do was to ask, believe and accept... They had to callout for help with utter faith and trust that Spirit was there to help them! And once they did, Help would reach out every single time!

I couldn't help but think, that this was also true for the lost Souls back on Earth. (before they committed suicide) All they had to do was ask for help and believe that everything was a gift in disguise, and brighter days were ahead...

Next, I was shown how the prayers of loved ones can help a lost Soul. Especially a Suicide Soul. I was reminded of some ancient cultures and their traditions like, 'All Saints Day'. Also known as Día de Muertos or Allhallowtide... In the Aztec tradition this was a ceremony that was associated with a celebration in the spring. Later in the 1600's, it gradually was associated with October 31, Nov. 1, and Nov. 2, to coincide with Western Christianity.

'The Day of the Dead', as it is often referred to today is celebrated throughout much of the world and is a positive gathering time for the family and friends of people who have died. These family members and friends believe their prayers, songs and laughter help support their loved ones during their spiritual journey and can help them find the Light - if they are lost or trapped along the way. Alters are built and photos of the loved ones are placed on the alters where they are prayed for, sung and spoken to with love.

I quickly saw how this focused power of prayer does in fact help lift the lost Souls into the Light. I watched how focusing loving intentions can divide the darkness and show the way to the Light for those who are lost along their journey.

I then thought about Hallows-Eve aka Halloween, and how so many dress up as ghouls and evil entities on Oct. 31. These are the same entities I saw floating in the Dark Abyss! This realization made me think about what I put out there with my actions and words… and it also made me question, "Is this a coincidence?"

I think the tormented faces in the abyss were actually the faces of the lost soul's own guilt and sorrow. Because when these Souls let go of their own torment, they were free to soar to the Light! I came to see this applies to those both on Earth and those in the Hell-like Grey Void as well.

What I witnessed next was a summary of events of when someone commits suicide. It went something like this...

- First the Spirit commits suicide and dies...
- Then they leave their body and will choose to either go directly to the Light or they may choose to flounder in the Darkness for what can feel like an eternity.
- If they choose to swim in the Darkness for a period of time, they will feel trapped – but they aren't. They are in essence experiencing a guilt-ridden, darker life-review of torment. It's not a pleasant experience and can be filled with pain – both physically, mentally and emotionally.
- When the Spirit feels worthy enough, or is willing to accept the Light, they will immediately travel out of the abyss and into the Light with ease.
- Everyone eventually comes to the Light. Prayers from the lost Soul and from their loved ones, help greatly in the Soul's advancement.
- I saw that the Darkness is another loop within the loop of life. It's like you spiral downwards into a lower vibration when you choose this second route.
- The Darkness can feel like quick-sand to the trapped Spirit. Fear can hold the Soul in place.
- Some Souls have great difficulty emerging from their depths of despair that they have clung to – like an old dysfunctional friend.
- But when they seek the Light, Help shall appear.
- The Soul may avoid the dark abyss all together. And instead travel directly into the Light upon the act of suicide – avoiding all the agony. (It seems to depend on their level of 'worthiness' to which route they

choose)

- Once in the White Void, the Suicide Soul will review their life.
- They will discover the missing lesson(s) they need to focus on.
- The Soul and Spirit will be able to rest and recoup until they feel united again and strong enough to return.
- And once ready – they are sent back to start their same life experience all over again.

I remembered thinking to myself, "What? Start all over again??? But how? How could they repeat their same life? Because once they're dead, they're dead, right??" The Elder smiled again and said, "Think beyond the linear."

I didn't get what he meant by this… (It was 1993 after all). I was stumped! So he continued, "The (Suicide) Soul will return and enter back into the Earth Realm to relive their lifeline all over again. With their same parents, the same situations, same joys and challenges. They'll live their life all over again in a parallel dimension. Which then creates a loop within a loop of life.

I saw that no matter what kind of decisions the Soul makes in each version of his/her life on Earth, they'll ultimately arrive at the same point where they have committed suicide once, twice, or a thousand times before. They'll be given the same choices to make each and every time – to either commit suicide again and again and again; or they'll find enough strength to overcome their hurdles – thereby closing the loop and ending the cycle of hitting the cosmic repeat button.

Immediately, I thought about a movie that had just been released at the time called, "Groundhog Day". It was a movie about a man who was caught in a time-loop – constantly reliving the same day over and over again. The day always started with the same song, "I got you babe". This was a great foreshadowing moment 'to just trust', I thought to myself.

Well, in the movie the lead actor Bill Murray soon discovered no one else was aware of this repeating loop he was in, but him! He indulged in a few one-night stands, did some binge drinking and even committed suicide a couple of times. But he could never escape the loop of waking up to the same song and starting his day all over again. Over and over again! After a while, he got past his frustration and began to accept his circumstances. He started to learn languages and even committed the odd random act of kindness. His love for life grew, until the day he chose to live differently once and for all.

On THIS day, Bill's character exclaimed – not only was he in love with the woman of his dreams, but he LOVED himself as well! It was at this moment he broke the repeating loop pattern and woke up to a brand-new life.

Referring to this movie, I asked the Council of Men, "Is this what our time on Earth is all about? Learning to live in a space of unconditional love and gratitude? Because right now, I'm past the binge drinking and self-loathing stage... Today, I'm more in the 'learning another language' and 'how to dance' stage. I'm not in love with myself fully yet... I know that. But I am in love with Michael."

I continued with my questions, "So does this mean that because I died at 29, I'm now in a 29-year loop? Will I repeat this life over and over again, until I can forgive and love myself unconditionally? And did I use an 'exit strategy' of a heart attack to come have this rest, instead of suicide? Does this mean I have to go back to start all over again? Or do I start again where I left off?

The Elder just smiled and calmly said, "It's complicated. Yes, you are not dead, so there is no starting over for you. This is more like having a very close call that has startled you to change. You are not dead, nor are you alive. You can still make a choice of whether to stay here or not. The option is open to you."

Ultimately, by no longer choosing suicide and instead choosing life over death, the Suicidal Soul will see that all those mountains in their life – that they once felt were insurmountable, were just molehills.

Once they let go of their emotional hurdles and move on, they'll look back and question why they thought those obstacles were so difficult in the first place... Eventually, they'll create healthier thoughts and when they come to the end of their lifetime on Earth, they'll celebrate! Shouting to the heavens! "Yes! I did it!"

The Elder paused and then added, "The act of suicide creates an abrupt fracture in the grid or matrix of your timeline, and this is why many experience déjà-vu" (translated as 'what you've already seen before') He said, "Suicide creates a skip in your record of life. And as a result, you'll see repeated events in your timeline. You'll likely say to yourself, "I've been here before!" This is because you have! Over and over again… And you'll continue in this repeating loop until the blessed day when you decide to grow past that moment of suicide or deep despair, or premature deaths, and embrace life fully.

The Elder reminded me that, "Whenever you sense a deja-vu, be aware of what you are doing and thinking at the time, because this is where you have a fracture in your matrix. Once you understand that you've injured the grid somewhere along the way, you'll find through compassion and forgiveness for yourself (and others) that you can energetically heal this 'glitch' in your grid. Thereby healing everything and everyone around you."

The Elder then said, "After suicide, you always return to your life with the intention to get past where you quit before, but it can take many attempts to heal and find the faith to move past that pivotal point, without self-harm. Seldom does a Spirit complete its growth cycle without having to make several attempts at doing so".

The Elder added, "This is what a deja-vu is… It is your Soul remembering that it's been here before. It's the memory of doing these actions over and over again in parallel dimensions. Rarely does a Soul complete their entire lifetime in one fell swoop, because Earth is one of the most challenging of planes. It requires great trust and faith to masterfully get from the beginning of one's lifetime to the end. Some are able to live through their lives with ease and grace, no matter how difficult their challenges are. And they do this because they are open to all solutions – no matter how they may appear. They ask for help or guidance often, and they accept the answers that are given – even if the solutions at the time may not make sense or may not come in the form they think is best. They trust that in the end, every reply is a gift from the heavens."

Next came a Lesson in Time…

CHAPTER 16

WHAT IS TIME

I turned to the entire group of the Council of Men and asked, "So how can you restart your life all over again with all the same people if they are still living a life without you on Earth?"

The Head of the Council replied, "Good question. In the simplest of terms, time is not what you perceive it to be. In the existence of the Earth Plane, time is perceived to be linear... Flowing East to West. (While explaining this concept, the Elder stretched out his arms to his sides and suddenly a golden beam of light appeared horizontally between his two hands. The beam stretched out about 5-6 feet in length) The Elder continued speaking while using this light beam to make his point... He said, "As a human, you will see time with a start, a middle and a finish. This is an illusion that was necessary for your spiritual growth. Instead, time is like this!" Suddenly the golden beam of light rotated and became vertical! Straight up and down!

The Elder said, "This is what time is like… North to South. Up and Down. Where the Past, Present and Future are all happening at the same time. You may feel on Earth as if you are on the planet for years and years, but in effect, it is but a moment of time. That is why we say, "All you have is the Now… You see?" He questioned.

There is no time other than the moment you are presently in – at this very moment. Those open enough to this principle can simply jump in and out of the timeline. They can either observe or even alter their timeline as the Observer. This is because with every decision, word and thought you make, you alter your timeline's direction… Which then effects your pathway and ultimately your level of growth."

I asked the Elder, "Can you turn your life around completely? It's not all pre-destined, right?" "Of course," he said. You already have the most marvelous lifetime ever written for you - it's waiting for you to be lived and embraced… It has been designed specifically for your spiritual journey and growth. You'll find you will have similar beginnings and midpoints - but your ultimate celebrated ending is up to you."

He added, "It's like a maze. There are many routes to take. Instead of celebrating these options, many see life as a labyrinth. They can only see one way in and one way out." The Elder concluded, "You may give up from time to time, but ultimately the better your thoughts and intentions are, the greater your outcome is. Your options are limitless! With endless blessed ways in and out of every situation or circumstance."

Creator then spoke, "Within your life's time, the truth about time and energy will be revealed. You can live simultaneously in many parallel dimensions and universes. You may not understand it yet, but in your timeline, you will."

God then said, "It appears you still have some self-doubt. We are here to reassure you that you are perfect in every way, as are all living-beings, in all places and all times. Please have faith. Simply come from a place of harmony and love. Simply be, and it will be.

Listening to Creator's message, I began to think about another Beatles song "Let it Be." God began to smile again, having seen (and heard) my thoughts. He said, "Indeed, yes... let it be.

With a clap of his hands, he concluded our meeting and said, "So let us return you to Earth then, shall we? Where you may enjoy all the gifts given. Yes?" God asked. I thought for a moment, and said, "Um... No thank you. I'd like to stay here please. I appreciate all that you've shared with me, but I don't want to go back." There was silence, as the Members looked at one another. This was apparently not what they wanted to hear... I really wanted to stay in the Light, but would they let me?

"When you let go of who you are, you become who you might be"
By Rumi

CHAPTER 17

GOING HOME

After all these insights and lessons in the White Void, I felt such deep love and gratitude for my life, and the gifts I had been given. I said to all the Men at the table, "Thank you so much, but I don't want to return to earth. I love the feeling here! This is much better... I'd like to stay here please."

God said, "Yes, there have been many lessons learned here. Now that you have recalled this knowledge, you can return with new strength and continue your path of contribution." I looked at Creator and without hesitation I chuckled and answered, "No thank you... I want to stay here." God smiled and said, "You are a beautiful Soul and you must return because you have much to do on Earth." Another Council Member interrupted and agreed saying, "Yes, you have much to do. It is time for you to return my dear."

I looked at the members of the Council of Men and thought about my fiancé Michael back on Earth. I asked, "Michael will be back here with us all soon, right? And like you said, there is no time, so he won't miss me much back on Earth, right?"

I could see the members energetically huddling together to have a private conversation. The Elder broke away from the group and announced, "You're on a new path, and will accomplish much. Please trust us… It is time to return."

Getting frustrated I threw my arms up in the air and said, with a bit of a sarcastic voice, "Oh my God! What worldly good could I do that would be so significant back on Earth, that I need to return for? I'm illiterate! I can't read! I was placed in the dummy class in grade 8 and failed grade 12! I have no education! I'm a bartender! And an alcoholic! PLUS! I can't even have any children!!! What good will I ever accomplish?"

The Members looked at me with such patience... The head of the Council smiled and said, "It is rare that we reveal what we are about to show you, but we feel it is in the best interest for you to see this."

To my right, two small golden white holograms appeared and floated beside me. In the center of the spheres, I could see images beginning to appear. And just like before, I was sucked into both Holograms as soon as I looked at them! I had the sensation of being divided into two people with one mind… I could see, feel and sense what was going on in both holograms - simultaneously!

I saw a beautiful little girl in the first hologram. And another equally beautiful little girl in the other. One was blond and the other was brunette. Instantly, I understood that these were my future daughters! Both had their father Michael's piercing blue eyes, and joyful smile. I was playing with each child and watched as our smallest daughter was being lifted up and tossed in the air by my partner… She was giggling with such joy! This little blonde one also loved to cook! I saw glimpses of her cooking with me in the kitchen. She'd climb up on her stool with her chef's hat on, and together we'd make dinner.

Meanwhile, I was also watching our oldest daughter in the other Hologram. She was the brunette daughter and appeared to be about 2 years old at the time. She was also giggling so! She was running through our sprinkler system and was spraying me with water. Together we laughed and I picked her up, hugged her and spun her around with such joy! The next vision I saw was of her a few years later... I was teaching her how to write the alphabet by dotting the letters for her to trace. She was just so darn smart and listened so well with such enthusiasm.

They both were extremely bright! I had such an overwhelming love for both our girls! I remember thinking to myself, "Oh my God, I'm going to be a Mom! I get to have children!" As I watched these interactions with our future children, I could hear God's voice say, "You need to return... You have so much to do."

I immediately turned away from the images of my girls and came zooming back out of the Holograms. I could barely contain myself! I said to God, "Ok... You've got me! You always knew I wanted children! And I'M GOING TO BE A MOMMA!" I cheered and begged! "I wanna go back right now please! Can I?"

Instantly, I found myself standing on the edge of Heaven... God was at my side, and the Council and Jesus were in the distance behind Him. I was looking down at the beautiful blue green planet we call Earth. I quickly said good-bye and thank you to everyone. Then I turned back to the outer-limits. I was about to take the largest swan dive of my life - off the edge of Heaven and towards Earth! I took a deep breath in... And just as I was about to leap, God grabbed me energetically by the shoulders and said, "Before you go, there is one more thing."

"There is nothing either good or bad, but thinking makes it so."

By William Shakespeare, Hamlet

CHAPTER 18

THE FIVE LESSONS

Creator said, "There's one more question we'd like to ask you, before you return to Earth." I was puzzle yet agreed. God said, "If you were to ask us a question... any question, what would that question be?"

I was dumbfounded! I didn't have a clue how to answer such a profound request. Within seconds, a brilliant tiny white light came zigzagging out of nowhere and darted straight for my head! Before I could duck it entered directly behind my right ear - in the soft part of the skull. I felt it enter my brain and go straight into the center of my mind! Instantly, I had that spark of energy! It was like a light bulb moment went off in my brain! And instantly I knew exactly what question to ask...

I looked at God and without hesitation I said, "I've got it! I've heard that God loves everyone… Including the rapists, murders, molesters, and people who do the most heinous acts on Earth. But how? And why? How is it that you can still love someone who does so much to hurt others?" God smiled and said, "Oh, that's an easy one... Like this." And as he waved his arm from the right to left, I was instantly transported into another time and place!

I found myself suddenly standing up and hovering about a foot off the floor in another section of the White Void. It felt like a room without walls. I looked around and discovered I wasn't alone... There were two other Spirits in this 'room'. It suddenly dawned on me what this was... This was one of my own memories! It was when I was sitting with my 'Spiritual Guidance Counsellor' just before I came to Earth. I could see a younger version of myself sitting at a white desk with a non-gendered, almost robotic looking Counsellor. Together they were talking about my upcoming entry into the Earth Realm. They were planning what emotions and lessons I wanted to learn from during my time on Earth.

It was the strangest experience because everyone seemed to be aware that I was hovering in the room, yet they ignored me. I watched as the Counsellor suddenly got up and stepped out of the 'memory' as she approached and acknowledged me. She introduced me to my younger looking self by saying, 'Memory Self' please meet your 'Observer Self', and 'Observer Self', this is your 'Memory Self'. Ok then, now that you've met, let's begin." And with that, we all stepped back into the memory, and I began to observe the most interesting conversation ever!

The Counsellor's authoritative voice cut the silence rather sharply as she reviewed the summary of our agreement. An open dialogue began between the three of us and it went something like this...

The Counsellor: "Okay then, let's review what we have for you, and what experiences you've chosen so far. Your name will be Carrie Louise, and you will be born sickly. You'll have kidney stones for the first fourteen years of your life, and at age 3... you'll be molested."

Memory Self: "Yes! Fantastic!!! That's awesome!"

Me (Observer Self): "Oh my God! Excuse me! But did I just get really happy about being molested??? Are you kidding me?"

The Counsellor stood up and immediately the memory froze. Nothing moved! The Counsellor approached me again and spoke... "Yes, your Memory Self did celebrate, because she remembers what you have forgotten... She recognizes the opportunities that will arise from these and other experiences. With every experience you have on Earth, you will have the opportunity to apply the '5 Lessons of Life'.

Me (Observer Self): The 5 lessons of life?

The Counsellor: "Yes, with every experience you have, you will have the opportunity to apply the 5 Lessons of Life which are, unconditional love, forgiveness, faith, trust, and compassion."

Seeing I was still drawing a blank, the Counsellor continued...

The Counsellor: "With each experience, good or challenging, you can apply these 5 Lessons. Your Memory Self remembers that this is the key to your Spiritual Growth on Earth. First you need to apply the 5 Lessons of Life. And to see if you've applied them properly, you'll need to ask yourself a series of simple questions. For instance, if someone has hurt you physically or emotionally, then you'll ask yourself:

- Do I love this person unconditionally?

- Do I forgive them?

- Do I have faith they are (or were) in my life for a reason?

- And do I trust that our experiences together will serve the collective moving forward? (In other words, "Do I trust everything happens for a reason?")

- And lastly, do I have compassion for them?

"If you can answer 'yes' to all of these questions, then you are doing well in moving forward in your growth. But if you answer 'no', then you must apply the 5 Lessons of Life more effectively."

The Counsellor added: "These questions are not just applied to those Souls you perceive to be outside of yourself. They must also be applied to your own Self as well. For instance, in using the same example of being hurt by someone... it is best you ask yourself:

- Do I love myself unconditionally?

- Do I forgive myself unconditionally for all that I've said or done.

- Do I have faith that I am on the right path?

- Do I trust that everything has happened for the best possible outcome?

- And do I have compassion for myself in all ways?"

Again, if you answer 'No' to these questions, then it is time for you to shift your way of thinking. To welcome and practice that which is lacking... Love, Faith, Trust, Forgiveness or Compassion. The ultimate goal is to feel completely grateful for everyone and everything - including yourself."

The Counsellor paused and asked: "Do you understand?"

Me (Observer Self): I nodded, and while digesting it all, I began to daydream – thinking back to my time on Earth. I had spent much of my life beating myself up emotionally and verbally, saying things like, "How could I be so stupid? Man, I'm such an idiot! or I'm too fat, or too skinny (I used to yoyo with weight) or too short, or too, too, too..." I certainly didn't have compassion for myself. Nor did I forgive or love myself unconditionally. And by no means did I feel I was on the right path until that fateful day of my first death... when I prayed so hard for help! That was my turning point. When everything started to get better. Could it have been because I changed my thought process? And intuitively began practicing the 5 Lessons of Life without even knowing it?"

I brought my focus back to the Counsellor who was still

observing me. We both smiled at each other, and I could sense she was watching and listening to all my thoughts. I then had another insight and asked myself, "Hey, are these actually my thoughts or are they hers? Is she influencing and directing my mind?" I looked at the Counsellor and she just turned around and walked away... She stepped back into the suspended memory and reassured me by saying, "The 5 Lessons of Life will make more sense as we progress. Now let's continue."

The memory started back up and once again we were creating a life plan for me to live on planet Earth...

"In every minute you are angry, you lose 60 seconds of happiness"
Ralph Waldo Emerson

CHAPTER 19

CHOOSING PARENTS

The Counsellor took her seat again and immediately the memory unfroze. My Memory Self and the Guidance Counsellor continued with the summary of my life's choices. The Counsellor said, "Fine then. Let's look at your parental options, shall we?"

Another 9D hologram quickly appeared and hovered to our right. This time the hologram became a projector! Two people appeared above the sphere, in a holographic image. I recognized these two right away! They were my parents! The Counsellor greeted them and asked, "Would you like to be Carrie's parents?" My Mom's face beamed as she said in the kindest of voices, "Oh yes, we would be so pleased to be her parents." My father smiled in agreement. And with glee my Memory Self shrilled with joy and excitement!

Immediately, I had a deep level of concern as I interrupted and asked... "Excuse me, but doesn't my Memory Self have any concern about my Dad's drinking years? It wasn't the most pleasant of times after all. Don't get me wrong, Dad was an amazing man, but when I was young and he drank, Dad's temper would fluctuate vastly. It wasn't fun."

The Counsellor understood my concern and again froze the memory. She said, "Yes, your Memory Self understands the rage your father feels (and felt), but she also understands its origins. She knows he will heal and will become the man he is meant to be through practicing the 5 Lessons of Life."

The Counsellor added: "Your Memory Self is open to applying the 5 Lessons of Life, and because of this... she is thrilled to have these opportunities to discover and grow from applying faith, trust, compassion, forgiveness and love in every situation."

The concept was starting to settle into my mind...

The Counsellor continued: "Okay then. Let's now discuss the rest of your choices, shall we? Including when you'll be molested."

I couldn't help myself... I objected yet again.

Me (the Observer Self): "Now this is going too far! Are you really saying that I'll be happy about being molested on Earth? Are you kidding me??? I can't even say the word... mo - lested. Ugh!"

The Counsellor hushed me and asked that I trust her and just observe. I shook my head, crossed my arms, and watched in shock what came next...

CHAPTER 20

SOUL PAK

The Counsellor brought my attention back to the hologram once again. We said good-bye to my future parents, and they disappeared along with the hologram. I knew what was to come next and felt so uncomfortable! I wondered if another hologram was about to pop up with my two molesters in it... "Would I have to choose them too?" I thought sarcastically to myself!

To my surprise, twelve 6-foot-tall 'Light Beings' began to float into the brilliant White Room. They gathered behind the Counsellor and Memory Self and stood opposite from where I was hovering. Immediately, I thought of the movie Cocoon... Where the ETs unzipped their human body-suits and revealed they were Light Beings underneath. Well, these 12 Enlightened Beings were now standing right in front of me! They also had the same 5-point star shape of humans. They had a head with 2 arms and 2 legs and were radiant! They simply glowed with energy…

Almost on cue, the Counsellor turned to me and explained, "This is your Soul Pak. You have travelled with them from lifetime to lifetime, trading positions or roles in many lives. Sometimes one will be your mother, or father, babysitter, teacher, wife, husband, child, neighbor or best friend. When meeting them on the Earth plane, there will be an instant sense of familiarity with these Souls. You will often feel that you have known each other forever. This is because you have.

I asked why we have Soul Paks, and the Counsellor said, "The reason why you travel with the same primary pack of Souls from lifetime to lifetime, is because by doing so - you'll spend less effort getting to know each other, and more time learning from the experiences and lessons you've chosen to share with one another."

The Counsellor brought our attention back to my Soul Pak, and while addressing them she questioned, "So which two of you would like to be Carrie's molesters?" Immediately, two of the brightest Spirits raised their arms and exclaimed with enthusiasm, "We will!"

My Memory Self once again burst out in delight! She clapped her hands and thanked the two Spirits with everything she had! My Memory Self brought her hands together in front of her as if she were praying, and with the deepest sense of gratitude she said to these two volunteers, "Thank you... so much!" My Memory Self seemed to see this as the most incredible gift she could have ever been given by these two members of her Soul Pak!

That was when I had just about enough! I stepped up and said, "Alright, I've got to object!" The Counsellor interrupted and shushed me yet again. She firmly stated, "Please! Just watch."

Immediately the two magnificent Light Beings took flight and flew up and over us. They both dove off the edge of Heaven and sped towards their new homes on the Earth plane. They flew at lightning speed and ZOOMED down towards the Earth! It was then, I realized every one of us in the White Void's room were watching them. We were all connected to these two volunteers - we could see, feel, hear and sense everything they were going through.

I felt both Souls as they entered into each of their mother's warm wombs. Immediately we could hear the verbal abuse surrounding both of them. The screaming and fighting of their families. We could feel these volunteer's experiencing extreme terror before they were even born! One of them was even inebriated much of the time from the alcohol consumed by his mom.

After their births, we could see and feel the sexual and physical abuse they went through... from birth, right into their teens. We could understand all the decisions they made out of self-preservation and learned behavior. And in their late teens, we witnessed the two of them meeting and coming together as a couple.

We fast forwarded through their 20's, and into their 30's. They were now in their early 40's when they travelled from Europe and came to meet and groom my parents. They met our family in a campground in southern Ontario. Unbeknownst to us, they were producers of child pornography and wrote for an underground European magazine in the late 1960's. I was only three years old when they first saw and targeted me.

We all watched remotely from the White Room as the couple built a relationship with my parents over the next year. We watched as they convinced my Mom that she deserved a break from caring for us kids. They told her she had been "cooped up for far too long on the remote military base". They insisted they would take care of me for a weekend and give my Mom some well-deserved time to herself.

We watched as my Mom reluctantly decided to take advantage of this offer. She planned her trip to travel south to Montreal, where she was going to visit family there for the first time in years. I could also see how hard this decision was for my Mom. She had never been away from the kids in 13 years… Not even for a day!

We in the White Void, watched as my mom decided to take advantage of this 'nice' couple's offer. They would take me to the lake for the weekend while my brother (13) and sister (10) stayed with my Dad - and got to know him better. We watched as my Mother walked from our house, carrying me on her hip, out to the couple's car. My Mom reluctantly handed me over to the attractive woman in the front seat. Immediately I began to scream, kick and desperately reached for my Mom! I didn't want to go!

We could feel my Mom's heart breaking as she turned around and quickly walked back into the house... trying to conceal her tears.

Next, we watched as this couple drove us to my adopted Grandfather's vacant cabin on the lake – not far from our military base. Colonel Edwards was his name. He had a tiny cabin located deep in the woods of Northern Quebec that we could use whenever we wanted.

We all watched from the White Void as the couple and my 3-year-old-self arrived at the lake and began to unpack for our weekend away.

The woman appeared to be kind, and I saw my little-girl-self being dressed by her as I got into my favorite bathing-suit. I was painfully shy, so the woman took me by the hand and coaxed me out of the house, onto the deck - where she showed me off to her husband. "Look at our little princess! Isn't she lovely?" The woman asked. Her husband turned around briefly and agreed. I saw the man had a camera in his hands and was taking photos of the surroundings. He then turned towards me again and bent down. He smiled and asked in a sweet voice, "Can I take your picture?"

(As the 'Observer Self', I knew a little bit of what was to come next, but I only remembered up to a certain point. I think it's God's way of protecting the mind from such horrific trauma. You just simply forget)

We (in the Void) continued to watch as the man asked me to pose like Wonder Woman in my cute little bathing suit. We could hear his camera begin to click and slide over, and then click some more. We could feel his intentions. He was trying to get me to relax for this first set of photos. But just as the next set of photos were about to be taken - where I was about to be brutally raped, the vision we were all watching STOPPED!

Everything froze! And it was completely silent...

I quickly turned around to look at the Counsellor in the Void. I wanted to see why everything had stopped. "What happened?" I asked her! "I don't remember much about this attack... I always remember up to a certain point, but nothing after that! I want to know what the hell he did, so I can finally get over this pain!"

The Counsellor got up from her desk and came over to me. The rest of my Soul Pak were standing closely behind her. She said, "The full memory will be revealed to you when the time is right. But for now, it is our intention that you focus on what the 5 Lessons of Life and your Soul Pak are all about?"

She said, "Don't you see? These two had to be your best friends here, in order to do what they just did... They volunteered to live an incredibly challenging life - knowing this would give you the greatest opportunity to apply the 5 Lessons of Life! It's one of the most self-less acts they could have given you, for your greatest growth..."

I had no words. I just stood there stunned! The silence was deafening, and my ears were ringing. Had I not seen this with my own eyes, I don't know if I could have digested what was being shared... "You mean to tell me that my molesters were my best friends in Heaven?" Wow! I was gob-smacked!

I struggled to process this information. I looked over at the remaining 10 members of my Soul Pak. They were all so beautiful and loving. I thought about these two Spirits back on Earth, and how just moments ago they were standing in front of me as part of our Spiritual Family! They were beaming and had nothing but love in their Souls. Yet on Earth... they were far from Angelic.

The more I digested what had just happened, the more I felt it had to be true...

"Our greatest enemies are actually our best friends in Heaven!"

It made sense after all! When we experience anger, hate or violence, it automatically feels crappy. But when we train our brain to choose a more positive reaction, it does our Soul good! I thought to myself, "It's true! Because you can actually feel your heart and Soul expand when you choose Love in the most trying of circumstances."

I began to question myself, "Could this be the reason why we are all here on this planet? Is it to apply the 5 Lessons of Life in every situation we have?

Is this our Divine Directive...
To love and grow our Spirit within?"

I then saw moments of how I too had been both kind and cruel to others on Earth. I watched myself and cringed at some of the mean things I had done... but with each event, I noticed that I too was giving those Souls great opportunities to practice the 5 Lessons of Life as well. Now this is no excuse to go out and be cruel. In fact, I believe our entire directive is the complete opposite. It does, however, give you the freedom to forgive yourself and all others concerned when you've been cruel, or received harmful words or experiences. That, I believe is why we are all here. To choose love, compassion, forgiveness, faith and trust in all that we do, say and think!

I then heard the Counsellor's words say, "Indeed! Your Spirit would not be this magnificent, strong, compassionate and loving, had you not gone through everything you have in your lifetime. It is through your tragedies that you can experience the greatest growth. Immediately, I heard my Mom's words,

"Today's tragedy is tomorrow's blessing"
Doreen Laurent

With that, I came to comprehend my Mom's profound wisdom on a whole new level. The Counsellor smiled and said with a tenderness in her voice, "It's time for you to return now."

Instantly, I was back at God's side on the edge of Heaven... I was ready to go home with these profound secrets - that I intended to tell as many people about, as I possibly could. But would God let me? Or more so... would I find the courage to let myself speak this truth?

"At some point, you just gotta forgive the past, your happiness hinges on it" - Aaron Lauritsen

CHAPTER 21

THE PHOENIX

It was as if the entire Universe had been explained to me. I could see the greater truth that it all comes down to love... Love of others. Love of matter and non-matter, Love of Self, and everything else in between! Just Love! I was also shown how we can best apply this love - by applying the 5 Lessons of Life... By being aware of our thoughts, and how powerful we are through (and with) them. By knowing Help is always here – so just ask for it. To remember to live consciously in Gratitude. AND through asking better questions of yourself and others - while using the Cosmic Garbage Can...

As this understanding became clearer, so did my visions. Soon I found myself being transported out of this memory and before I knew it, I was back in the presence of God again! We were standing together on the edge of Heaven... exactly where

I had seen him last.

God greeted me and said in the warmest of voices, "Did this answer your question?" I laughed and said, "Boy did it ever! I'm leaving here with more knowledge than I could have ever wished for! Can I keep all of these insights?" Creator said, "Yes. You will remember much, but what is forgotten, will come back to you in the appropriate time."

I gave God the biggest hug good-bye and thanked him. He smiled and said, "It is time for you to go now my dear. You have so much to do and give. We are always with you and are ever present. Remember, it is as you experienced in the holograms. You are multi-present and purpose-filled. Time is not what you think. All is happening simultaneously, the past, present and future. So, enjoy, go, grow, and live this opportunity to its fullest!"

Creator gave me one last gift. He raised his hand up and extended his arm out in front of himself and suddenly the word 'NOW' appeared at the end of his fingertips. It was brilliant golden in color. God said, "And most of all, remember to live in the Now." He then gave a flick of his fingers, and the letters shifted! They spun around and spelled the word "WON." Creator smiled and said, "Because by living in the Now, you have Won."

I couldn't help but laugh as I joked and said, "So what does that mean about your name?" Creator chuckled and patted me on the back. I hugged God and said, "Thank you again. I'm ready to return 'Now' ha ha." I laughed again over my play on words – thinking I was oh so witty.

Looking at God one last time, I took a deep breath. I breathed in this experience of love, beauty, wisdom, and compassion. I closed my eyes and made a promise to myself that I'd always remember this... And with this last thought, I leaned forward and dove off the edge of Heaven!

Oddly enough, I didn't flail around or panic in this free-fall. I intuitively knew to just look forward as I sped through the clouds like a torpedo! I was trusting I was safe, and I'd be back in no time at all!

I felt the rapid descent begin to slow down as I came closer to my city, then street, then house... I gently flew right through the rooftop of my house and into my bedroom. Pausing for a moment, I looked at my lifeless body. It was still laying there - flat out on the bed... Surrounded by many half-filled moving boxes.

I decided to go ahead and re-enter my body. As I laid down facing up, I could feel the weight of my body again! I heard a rapid 'click, click, click' noise... It was the sound of my Body reconnected with my Mind and Spirit. I was back! Whole, Healed and One.

I still remember that first moment of opening my eyes. It felt like I was seeing the world through a completely different set of lenses! (And mindset for that matter) I was indeed back in my beautiful little suite in the hippy-dippy house in Kitsilano BC. Becoming reacquainted with my body, I began to move my fingers and toes... I stretched. It felt good to be back! My body felt a whole lot heavier than what I remembered... But my Spirit felt lighter and more free!

As my eyes adjusted to the earthly light, I heard rustling outside my bedroom door. Soon the pocket door slid open, and there stood three of my roommates, Myron, Megan and Marc! They came with gifts in their hands and were singing a song for me! I couldn't believe the words that came out of their mouths... They were singing 'Happy Birthday' to me! Yes, I had totally forgotten that today was my Birthday! (In more ways than one I guess) They sang with the biggest smiles on their faces. The three of them walked into my room, holding onto a homemade chocolate cake that was lit up with 29 candles on it!

Once they finished singing, Myron said to me, "Here are three gifts for you Carrie. We know that you've always wanted to have your own helicopter... so here's a toy helicopter to 'lift' you up and bring you to new heights. So, you'll always remember your dreams."

"Secondly" Myron added, "Here's a drawing and story that Megan created for you, to show how much we all love you!" Well, I just about fell over because on the front cover of the home-made book was an image Megan had drawn and colored... It was a HUGE brown bird!

Megan then explained, "This is the story of a legendary bird called the Phoenix. Do you know it?" she asked. "No" I answered. "Well, it's a legend that I think is true... It's about a large brown bird who rises from the ashes to give birth to a new way of life." She smiled and added, "And this is what we hope for you in your new married life Carrie."

"Wow" I thought to myself. "This is the same brown bird who took me on the trip to the White Void!" I looked down and quickly said a silent thank you to the Phoenix, to God, Jesus, and the Counsel of Men. I knew they could hear me and were watching all of us. I looked back up and turned to Megan. Swinging my arms open, I gave her an enormous hug!

The hug didn't last very long however, because Marc interrupted us while clearing his voice. "Ahem!" he said. Marc began to talk in a fake British - almost regal accent. He said, "And lastly, my dear lady… May I present to you a regular ancient stone", he joked while bowing his head and handing a rock to me in his open palm. I accepted the small smooth stone. Marc stood up and while cupping the rock in both of our hands, he spoke about one of his insights. He said, "Stones like this one, hold five meanings for us all...

1. May they represent the earth we walk on

2. And the gifts we both give and receive along our travels

3. May they remind us to keep grounded no matter how far we fly.

4. May they also remind us of our connection between the Heavens and Earth

5. And finally... May we understand how great, yet fleeting our lives truly are. Especially, when we look at the age of this stone... Long after we're gone, this little rock shall remain and will witness many generations to come. Our kid's kids may hold onto this very rock. Who knows...

Marc paused, and then became more serious. He looked me straight in the eyes, softened his voice, and said, "So during your precious time here, may you choose to make an impact on this giant pebble we call Earth..." He paused and quipped, "Or not", as he dropped my hands and began to walk away. Everyone laughed, but I knew Marc's joke had more truth in it, than fiction.

I was dumbfounded at the outpouring of love from my three wise friends. Myron then said with excitement, "Make a wish Carrie!" I blurted out in laughter as I thought to myself, "This whole life is my wish! Coming back is my wish! I feel like the luckiest person on this planet! I'm so grateful to be home with my friends who I now see as my family."

Closing my eyes, I made a wish to marry Michael, and to have those two beautiful children I saw in Heaven's Holograms. Both girls! One brunette and one blond... I love them already even though I hadn't really met them yet. But then I remembered, I have met them! They were two of my remaining ten Soul Pak members! And soon they'll also be volunteering to come join us all in this adventure called "Life".

"We are our future generation's history class...
It is time to rewrite our future's history books to reflect
a gentler, more humane society" - CK

Chapter 22

CONFIRMATION

After returning from this second near-death experience in 1993, I pleaded for God to give me some sort of confirmation. I needed to know that these experiences had actually happened.

NO ONE I knew (outside of our hippy-dippy circle) ever spoke of quantum physics and nanotechnology back then. So yes, I needed confirmation that there was such a thing as parallel universes, dimensions, the matrix, and gridlines... I needed to know that this meeting with God and the Council of Men really did happen. I prayed a lot my first night back to Earth - for some sort of confirmation and within 24 hours it arrived!

I woke up the next day after my NDE and had to go to the Vancouver International Airport to pick up Michael. He had been in Calgary for the past 2 days on a quick business trip. I had spent the whole morning running errands, and I arrived at the airport nearly 2 hours before his flight arrived. With lots of time to spare, I wondered up to the top floor of the airport which was under construction. (This was pre 911 and you could wander around the airport without any questions or restrictions) The only shop built so far on the top floor was one very large bookstore. Even though I didn't read, I thought I'd go and check it out... Maybe I could find a colorful magazine or something to look at, to pass the time away.

As I approached the front entrance of the bookstore, I thought it was strange because the entire front wall of shelves were completely covered with 100 or more copies of one single book. It was called, "Embraced By The Light" by Betty Eadie, and it had a beautiful picture of an Angel on the cover... I laughed to myself, as I grabbed one of the books and said under my breath, "Well, I guess I'm supposed to look at you, aren't I?" I lifted one of the books off the shelf, and as I opened it up the book fell open to the chapter titled, 'The Council of Men'!

Well, I slammed the book shut and squealed in excitement! "Oh My God! Here's the confirmation!!! The Council of Men does exist!" I reopened the book again to the very same page! Even though I was a painful slow reader at the time, I was able to make my way through the first several pages of the chapter. I came to understand that Ms. Eadie had the same experience that I did! She also met with the Council of Men and had similar interactions and reactions to the experience.

I said a private thank you to Creator and took a sigh of relief while saying to Spirit, "I KNEW what I had experienced was real! Thank you, Dear Lord, for hearing my prayers and for sending me this confirmation…"

Just as I finished saying the deepest prayer of gratitude, I looked up and made eye contact with a rather rough looking man who was standing in the corner of the store and was just staring at me. He looked homeless and dirty. Suddenly, I felt extremely un-comfortable. I buried my head back into the book in fear that he would approach. I glanced up again and sure enough, I could see he was coming straight towards me. I dropped my head again pretending to read, but inside I was thinking, "Oh good God! Please, don't let him hit on me. Just let him walk right past me!"

My prayer was interrupted by the kindest of voices, warmly saying to me, "That's a great book… It's a true story you know." I looked up to see the same guy standing in front of me… but instead of seeing a homeless man, I saw he was the most radiant Soul. He had a wonderful light emanate from him. This stranger told me that he had been a homeless man in Seattle, Washington. He had "died" in the same alley he had lived in. He said he now works with children who are abused. "He does God's work."

I was truly amazed with his beauty. His eyes had the same look of kindness that I had witnessed in Heaven. Our conversation was quick and fleeting. He just wanted to give me confirmation that Betty Eadie's story was real, because he had experienced the same things during his death as well. He smiled, said goodbye, and left the bookstore. I placed the book back on the shelf and thought, "Gosh, I'd like to talk with him more." I quickly exited the bookstore, but the airport appeared to be completely empty! The entire upper floor looked like a huge empty warehouse because it was still under construction. And the man I had met had simply disappeared!

I closed my eyes and said a silent prayer to God, "Okay Lord, if this is real, I need you to have him walk towards me in a straight line as soon as I turn around." (This was in the days when I demanded of God; and needed to make deals with him in order to know he was real) So, I stood there expecting to hear a response from God, but there was no answer. Deciding to just trust, I took a deep breath and spun around... sure enough! The same man was walking in a straight line towards me. He greeted me laughing and saying in his Hispanic accent, "I guess we were meant to talk some more, yes?"

"YES!" I said with enthusiasm! I asked him more about his death and his work with abused children. He shared that he had wasted much of his life in misery and depression. When he returned here to Earth, he decided to do as much as he could for the community. Especially with the children who were either homeless or abused in the City of Seattle. He added, "Every city has this problem, but for me, I wanted to work within the city I knew best."

The man then wrote down his phone number and name for me. He said while handing me the piece of paper, "Hi, I am Hector. You can call upon me anytime. Maybe someday we can even work together!" I smiled and said "Yes! I'd like that very much!" I looked down and tucked the white piece of paper into my pocket. As I looked up to see that Michael's flight was arriving, I turned back to say good-bye. Once again, the kind man had disappeared! I could see the entire upper floor of the airport. It was empty! He had vanished!

I reached back into my pocket and the piece of paper was still there (but within 24 hours it had disappeared as well). So, I stood there in the airport alone. Dumbfounded! Knowing Hector couldn't have run that fast to the end of the corridors, I finally had to admit to myself - Hector was not from this world. He was an Angel.

It wasn't until many years later that I understood the deep connection I would have with this kind Spirit. It was through a close call with a 3-time convicted pedophile and our first daughter, when she was only two years old. The pedophile never got to our daughter, but his attempt to kidnap her ignited my path of being one of the foremost experts in our country on pedophilia. I ended up volunteering and helping to write and amend 14 laws to protect children from harm...
And I believe this Angel named Hector was with me every step of the way.

Chapter 23

THE GIFT!

So, this story doesn't end here...

Fast forward nearly eleven years and by now my birthday wish had come true. Michael and I were married for ten years, and we were blessed with the births of both of our girls. One brunette and one blonde... and yes, they both have their father's brilliant blue eyes.

Surprisingly, Mike and I had grown apart over the years, and we decided to separate over a glass of wine on my birthday in 2003. We sold our family home in Northern Alberta, and I bought my own home with the money I was now earning from selling Real Estate. This was a difficult time for our family, especially for our girls who were both still so young. But like my Mom would say, "Out of every tragedy comes many blessings and insights."

It was this thought that I kept in mind as I attempted to heal all of our hearts from the divorce. I tried so hard to help our girls' transition, but what I came to understand was that it was my own heart that was broken beyond repair. I seemed to have a huge gaping hole of sorrow inside me, from the broken dreams of our life together. And guilt about our girl's pain... I did everything to help our girls heal but didn't know how to begin to help myself.

One of my most significant moments of healing and great hope came by way of our youngest daughter Amelia, (who was barely three years old at the time). I was unpacking the 100 or so moving boxes in our spacious brand-new home. And even though our new place was cheery and bright inside, I was feeling down. I felt so alone and uncertain about the girl's and my future. I worried how I'd be able to care for our children and afford this house on my own. I had always thought I'd be married forever to Michael after all. Especially after witnessing glimpses of our future in the White Void - but it didn't turn out that way.

Surrounded by a mountain of moving boxes, I decided to take a rest from unpacking... Flopping myself onto our big, old comfy couch in our new living room, Amelia quickly came over and crawled up onto my lap. Wrapping my arms around her, she snuggled in and together we watched the children's tv show called Barney. Amelia slowly looked up at me and paused. It was clear she had something on her mind. She gingerly spoke and asked the most unusual question...

Amelia asked in the sweetest of voices, "Momma... have you ever had another girl other than me and Nikki before?"

The question threw me back, because no one knew of my secret other than my ex-boyfriend, my Mom, and Michael (who was now my former husband). I hadn't spoken about losing Penni in the past 11 years! So how could my little one know about her?

I hesitated and was tempted to mask the truth with a 'white lie'. But looking at her sweet face and into her beautiful blue eyes, I knew I needed to be honest with her - she could handle this truth... So, I swallowed hard and said, "Actually honey, yes, I had another daughter. Her name was Penni, but I lost her before she was born."

Immediately, old emotions started to bubble up, and I began to cry. Amelia saw my sadness. She suddenly jumped up, knelt on my lap, and while facing me, she threw her little arms around my neck and gave me the biggest hug!

Amelia then cuddled into the crook of my neck and gently whispered in my ear, "It's alright Momma. Don't be sad... I think I'm her."

The End.

THE 5 LESSONS OF LIFE

LESSON 1 - FORGIVENESS

The message of forgiveness is a simple one. It all starts from within.

So many people are reluctant to forgive because they see forgiveness as condoning an act of violence, or pain that was forced upon them. They believe that if they forgive, then they release the responsibility of holding the person accountable for what they did or said.

Forgiveness is more for you than anyone else... It's a release of the circumstances or events. It's a conscious decision to come to an agreement with both yourself and others that you will simply focus on the lesson, rather than on the story itself.

Many people think they have to forgive the other person or people, when in fact the first and only person they need to forgive is themselves. Remember, the other person is your best friend from the White Void and is giving you the opportunity to apply the 5 Lessons of Life.

Forgiveness frees your Spirit and enables you to soar! So set the intention that only kind words will be spoken from this day forth. Forgive yourself and forgive others for all the harsh actions, words and thoughts you've shared between you both... and then move on.

Love thyself, love thyself, love thyself.

LESSON 2 - COMPASSION

You'll notice that once you open up your heart to forgiveness, compassion will walk right in beside it. This is because forgiveness and compassion walk hand-in-hand. One is dependent upon the other to fulfil your experience of transforming your viewpoint on life. They rely upon one another because:

- Without compassion, there is no empathy.
- Without empathy, you cannot see the other's perspective.
- Without this perspective, the heart isn't open fully to all possibilities.
- And without an open heart - your Spirit cannot forgive, grow or advance.

Once you come from a place of compassion for yourself and others, you'll open up your heart and understand yours and other's "whys". You may not agree with the other person's actions, but at least you'll understand their motivation. And by doing so, you can offer them empathy for their words or actions through forgiveness.

An example of this was in my youth when I was bullied... After my NDE, I reached out to the town bully where I grew up, and discovered his 'whys'... Why did he pick on those who were smaller than him? Why was he so mean?

I discovered it was because he was brutally abused by his own father. I finally understood why he lashed out. Because anger was all he knew. Listening to his treatment at home made me feel such compassion for him. I forgave him instantly once I understood his journey. I believe now, he was doing the best he could with what he had been dealt in life. And through open communication, compassion, and forgiveness, we both gained an unexpected friendship. It was through compassion that all fear and anger were released. It was just that easy.

LESSON 3 - TRUST

Trust is a touchy-feely subject. It creates more emotions than any other of the 5 Lessons. Especially if you have experienced trust being broken.

Take a look at the word...

TRUST

In fact, write it down, because there are many clues to healing broken trust, in the word itself...

When trust is broken often people feel lost, despondent, and confused. Their sense of direction may be shattered, especially if it means the ending of a relationship.

We all enter this world as trusting and loving beings. When we experience our first heartbreak, it can send us spiraling into a tailspin of uncertainty, instability, and even deep depression. This is because trust, honor, joy, and integrity are natural to our Soul's essence... the darker our actions, thoughts and emotions, the further we are from being connected to Source Energy.

These heavy, lower vibrations are learned behaviors here on Earth. It is our mission and goal here to rise up above these emotions, and to do better. To trust and be trusted as a whole.

When I was in the White Void, I sat with Jesus. I don't remember much of our conversation - other than what he shared with me about the power of words... He said, "There are many clues in languages and communications. Look at the words you use. Analyze them and in doing so, more truth shall be revealed."

So, I did this with the word "Earth" and found many words within it, like Ear and Hear, and Heart and Hater. From this I learned our time on Earth is about listening more, especially to address the emotions of the heart... I then looked at more words like...

Release - which becomes - Real Ease
Disease becomes Dis Ease
Together is Two Gathered
Imagination = Image a Nation (of love)
Universe = Uni-Verse or One Song (Spirit Song)
The name Jesus reveals itself to be, Je suis (I AM)
Human in Latin is Earth or Ground – therefore…
Humankind is translated to Earth Kind = Kind Earth Beings
Love backwards is Evol
Nowhere becomes Now Here
Television = Tell-A-Vision
Television 'Programming' – is simply that
Planet becomes Plan-ET (which is another book to come)
Alcohol = Al Kohl aka Spirit Eater. Named 'Spirits' for a reason
Intoxicated broken down in Latin means, To Have or Be in poison
Believe = Be / Leave (Just Be and Leave all your worries behind)
Empowered is translated as, I'm Powered
Stressed Backwards is Desserts
Imperfect becomes, I'm Perfect!
Impossible of course becomes, I'm Possible!
And the Devil becomes Lived, when reversed

156

Then I looked at the word Trust... What I discovered was that when you've lost trust, you may feel lost inside - like you've come to a "T" in the road.

The key to finding your way back from not trusting or perhaps being untrustworthy yourself... is to decide what it is that YOU desire! Give your worries up to Spirit, and Trust.

Start journaling and put your feelings down on paper. Write release letters. And practice the 5 Lessons of Life daily - with your own mini-life reviews.

When feeling lost or confused, we often put up a wall around our heart. This is in an attempt to protect ourselves from the pain or being hurt again - but it ends up creating a barrier. This self-imposed 'Heart Wall' slows down productivity, decision making, and positive thought patterns. Plus, it also shuts down our ability to trust ourselves, and our intuition or inner knowingness. If we don't trust ourselves or our connection to Spirit any longer, then we shut down energetically and begin to Rust away!

Becoming frozen in Fear is the most common culprit to giving-up on ourselves and others. And this 'rusting away' can happen in our workplace, our relationships, with our bodies, and minds – all through the lack of Trust...

Along with your Body, Mind, and Spirit, you can also stagnate and move backwards in growth and strength. Soon the mindless acts of watching television, texting, social media, taking selfies, or playing on the computer becomes the norm. We can fall into the trap of rusting away and becoming zombie-like, sleepwalkers... 'The walking dead'.

I believe the greater desire for all of us, is to realize the gift that 'Trust' brings. I was never one to read the Bible, but since my NDE, I do believe there is much truth in all the ancient texts - whether it's the Bible, Quran or Tao Te Ching to name a few... I believe each book of faith has many insights and much to offer to those with an accepting and open mind. The messages are always simple... Simply Trust.

Trust and all will be provided to you.

If you could see how little unconditional trust is needed to create miracles in your life, you'd be shocked! Simply trust in the fact the Universe supports your every thought. And know that Spirit is conspiring to help you at every moment that you ask for assistance. You are never alone! Help is always here for you, and it begins with simply asking for help...

Think healthy thoughts to have a healthier life.

Think prosperous-filled thoughts for a more prosperous life!

And think happier thoughts for a happier life!

Just Think...

If you want a dramatic, hectic life then worry constantly... because 'worrying is praying for the negative to happen'.

But if you want to clean up your life? Then clean up your negative thoughts! It's just that easy.

Trust!

And when you trust unconditionally, without judgement − your whole world will change for the better...

LESSON 4 - FAITH

Many think faith and trust are the same thing but they're not. They have similar qualities, but Trust is of the heart, whereas Faith resides in the Spirit and Soul. The difference between the two is great, but again... they go hand-in-hand.

The more that Faith and Trust are applied together, the stronger they become. It is as if an internal bridge is formed between the Heart, Spirit and Soul when both properties are applied properly, and in unison. It is like you're lighting up your own internal and eternal flame, when the intention is set to activate both Faith and Trust together!

While thinking about this Lesson, I was given these words...

Faith is a noun

(A person, place, or thing – it's your natural essence)

Whereas...

Trust is a verb

(An action word - something you do)

Therefore…

"Trust is Faith in Motion

Faith is when your Body and Mind state to the Universe...

- I'm ready to Trust…
- I'm ready to give up control and allow my heart to open up.
- I'm ready, willing and able to fully acknowledge and embrace the connectiveness that already exists within my Soul, Spirit and Divine Presence.
- I AM opened to allow the Glory of God to enter my conscious Mind, as we step together into the knowingness that all is provided, all-ways.
- I Agree to allow Source Energy to permeate every cell of my being-ness with endless Love, Health and Abundance.
- I Accept the rich omnipresent substance of the Universe as being one with me - individualized as me, in the here and now.
- I Agree to walk, In the Light, Through the Light, and Of the Light - for the Best and Highest Good for all concerned!
- And in doing so, I shall live my life in Faith, Trust, Forgiveness, Compassion and Unconditional Love!
- I commit to practice the 5 Lessons of Life in my life with gratitude daily.
- I commit to a morning and/or evening ritual of reviewing my thoughts and actions each day. What does not serve me and others, I toss into the Cosmic Garbage Can. I faithfully focus on my Best Possible Thoughts - which open the doors to new and brilliant opportunities with ease and grace.

By living in a state of faith, you are stating to the Universe that you 'Trust' with an open heart. That you trust your path is for your highest good and your outcome is in perfect alignment with the Divine Order.

Just know that everything is in perfect harmony, and your mission is to use the gifts you've been given to contribute to the whole. Whatever quirky or unusual talent you may have – have Faith and Trust that you have this talent for a reason! Get creative and think of all the ways you can give back to your family, friends, and community, because this is where your own miracles begin.

When you seek to share love and joy - do this through the faith in your heart, and trust in your own abilities. You are never alone. This is where magic begins. Know this to be true...

LESSON 5 - UNCONDITIONAL LOVE (AND GRATITUDE)

As I thought (and prayed) about what to write for this lesson, I could hear Spirit's voice say, "We saved the best for the last! Because it is through love that every - thing is possible."

At hearing this, I vividly recalled moments where I've experienced unconditional love at such depths that miracles have happened. Like many, I've witnessed people miraculously heal broken bones and terminal illnesses overnight. I've witnessed the power of both individual and group prayers. (I call it prayers - but it's where people have used the 'focus of loving intentions' to manifest their desired outcomes)

I've come to realize that it's in these states of heightened love that people are unconsciously embracing and practicing the 5 Lessons of Life. They are walking in harmony with everyone and everything around them! In fact, if they had held onto any anger, hatred, or resentment inside - the very act of these miracles wouldn't and couldn't have occurred.

We must 'Let go and let God' as the saying goes. We must be TOTALLY open and come from a non-judgmental and unconditionally loving state of mind, body and spirit in order to have positive energy flow through and to/from us...

By consciously practicing unconditional love with the 5 Lessons of Life, you'll find your Spirit will naturally shift into the next level of heightened e-motions and higher vibrations. The place where energy is alive and utter gratitude is a way of life.

When you live in a consistent state of unconditional love and gratitude, there is nowhere else to go, but up... You have arrived! As in the Buddhist faith, 'You will have found Nirvana - where you are released from the effects of Karma, and the cycle of death and rebirth'... (Which was shown to me as the endless loop of life)

When the mass majority of us on Earth reach this state of consciousness (the tipping point) we will influence the whole to do the same. Like the 100th monkey... What one does, the rest will take interest and may follow naturally. So be the first in your family, or community to set the intention to contribute and share unconditional love in everything you do, say, and interpret to be true. Start with love for yourself and let it flow to others... Start today... ♡

And always remember the intention of this book.

To...

Love Thyself, Love Thyself, Love Thyself

And so it is…

GET IN TOUCH

Go to www.CarrieKohan.com for further information on Private and Group Spiritual Mentorship / Coaching Sessions. Plus, both Live and Online Courses with Carrie.

Carrie is removing this book, and all future books from Amazon Sales and is Offering them privately instead. Please go to www.CarrieKohan.com´s Store to get all future copies in print or digital form.

Subscribe and follow her free videos on YouTube:
https://www.youtube.com/carrie_kohan
https://www.youtube.com/carriekohan

Become a patreon member and receive Carrie´s bi-weekly inspirational videos, and join her on her quest to buy a castle in France! In return, you'll be helping Carrie and her nearly 18-year-old puppy Bella, in all their new Spirit Given and Driven Adventures. You'll also be the first to receive her newest insights and downloads, and even excerpts from her newest books!
https://www.patreon.com/carriekohan

If you've enjoyed this book, please pass it forward by gifting a copy to your family / friends or your local library donation program. Simply request your library to contact Ingram Spark Wholesalers – ISBN # 978-1-99928-600-2

Finally, all your reviews (on Goodreads) are greatly appreciated. Xo
https://www.goodreads.com/en/book/show/52798870

ABOUT THE AUTHOR

Article Written by Aspen Gainer for the Edmonton Examiner Wednesday, July 4, 2012

It's not very often you meet a woman who has changed the face of a country. Carrie Kohan-a 48-year-old Métis mother of two, a national child advocate, federal government witness and public spokesperson, is one of those rare gems.

In addition to changing Canadian law, Kohan founded Project Guardian and Mad Mothers Against Pedophiles (MMAP) in 1998.

"What MADD did for drinking and driving, I wanted to do for pedophilia and the protection of children," says Kohan. "I wanted to educate the public, change laws and create a better environment for our children."

It is easy to see why Kohan has received so many awards, the most recent of which is the IAAW's Dorothy Daniels Justice Award for Advocacy. The award was presented June 8, 2012, at the Edmonton Expo Centre at the 17th Annual Esquao Awards. The ceremony is held by the Institute for the Advancement of Aboriginal Women each year to honor the 'Angels Among Us', and the amazing contributions of women in the aboriginal community.

FIGHTING TABOOS

When Kohan first began her journey as a child advocate, pedophilia was a taboo subject. No one wanted to talk about it or acknowledge it. Kohan's work as a lobbyist and advocate was instrumental in changing fourteen laws in Canada that now protect children from harm.

Her legacies include Amber Alert; the Provincial and National Sex Offender Registries; the Child Protection Act [Online Sexual Exploitation]; an increase in the age of consent from 14 to 16; Lisa's Law; and amendments to the divorce act and immigration laws. Kohan is even the namesake of the "Carrie's Guardian Angel Law" which asks for a 20-year minimum sentence for serial predators and pedophiles.

Listening to Kohan's resume of advocacy gives you goosebumps. She is not a lawyer and in fact has a learning disability that makes it very difficult for her to read at all, although you would never know it. She has flown to Ottawa multiple times to debate against some of the top lawyers in Canada - and won.

"There's a lot of pressure and I'm usually the only non-lawyer that speaks as a Federal Government Witness in Ottawa," says Kohan. "I'm a stay-at-home mom who became so versed in stats about pedophilia that no one could beat me in debates."

Kohan began her journey towards advocacy in her early thirties. "It's amazing what can come out of you when you're pushed to your limits," says Kohan, "and that's what happened."

TERRIBLE ENCOUNTER

At 34, Kohan was a stay-at-home mother of a young daughter. She and her husband (they are now divorced) owned a home-building company. Once their baby came, he took care of the business outside of the home, while Carrie took care of what happened inside the home. But Carrie's life was about to change dramatically, with a terrible encounter.

Unknown to her at the time, Kohan's neighbor was a three-time convicted pedophile. One day he entered Kohan's home and attempted to take their daughter, who was two at the time and sleeping in her crib.

Kohan intervened and saved her daughter before he was able to harm her, but that was the beginning of Kohan's new path in life. From 1998, she spent two years trying to find others who were already advocating against pedophilia but found no one.

After the incident with the neighbor, Kohan moved to Calgary. One day she heard a news report about two young children being molested in their homes and knew it was time to take action.

TAKING ACTION

Carrie phoned the Premier's office (at that time the Alberta Premier was Ralph Klein) and told them that she wanted to start an awareness campaign for child protection.

Kohan received an outpouring of support from Premier Klein and his staff, and that was the beginning of her 14-year and counting career as child advocate.

CANADA'S ERIN BROCKOVICH

Kohan's life of dedicated philanthropic service really is the stuff movies are made of. She deserves her nickname, 'Canada's Erin

Brockovich'.

Kohan was surprised and obviously pleased about winning the Dorothy Daniels' Justice award. My daughter actually nominated me for it, so not only was it wonderful to be nominated within our aboriginal culture, but to also have my own daughter nominate me was heart-warming," says Kohan.

Her two daughters are already showing the same ambition and spirit of perseverance as their mother. In addition to excelling in school despite their learning disabilities which they share with their mother; the youngest sings and has won some major roles in film and commercials; While the oldest is also an accomplished singer and actress, and toured across Canada as Miss Teenage Canada, speaking about the issues of clean drinking water.

The message that Kohan most wants to emphasize to youth is that you really can do anything you want to with perseverance, dedication, hope and faith.

"I never thought as a stay-at-home mom with a learning disability that I would amend fourteen laws in Canada and debate against some of the best lawyers in our country... And win!" But Kohan says she felt her journey was "Spirit Driven and Given." She believed in her cause, has faith to face her fears and she has changed our country for the better as a result.

If you would like to know more about Carrie Kohan and her contributions to the welfare of our children, you can research her name or read the Canadian Gov't Hansard Reports below:

https://openparliament.ca/committees/justice/39-1/56/carriekohan-1/only/

(Below is a link from a 2003 interview and it's quite graphic in the dialogue re: pedophilia – so please don't have children present when watching it. The interview starts at 42:00 and is only a few minutes in length. It's a very good interview and shows you where we were, and how far we've come)

https://www.cpac.ca/episode?id=850221a1-106a-42cf-b2a2-7312a7aa2eb1

AWARDS:

Carrie Kohan has been the recipient of the:

1. 2021 Bronze Medal – Readers' Favorite International Book Contest – Religion/Spirituality & Philosophy

2. 2021 Readers' Favorite 5 STARS Reviews (6-time Winner)

3. 2015 International Rotary Integrity Award

4. 2014 The Fierce Woman Award for Inspiration

5. 2014 Fierce Woman of the Year Award

6. 2012 Queen Elizabeth II, Diamond Jubilee Medal for Out-Standing Service

7. 2012 Alberta Mother of the Year Award

8. 2012 Institute for the Advancement of Aboriginal Women (IAAW) Esquao Award – Dorothy Daniel's Award for Justice

9. 2010 YWCA Woman of Distinction Award for Justice

10. 2001 United Nation's 'Volunteer of the Year' Medal

11. 2001 Gov't of Canada's 'Volunteer of the Year' Medal

ACKNOWLEDGEMENTS

This book is first and foremost dedicated to the energy of God, Jesus, and the Council of Men. Thank you, thank you, thank you. When you said I had to come back because there was so much to do - you weren't kidding!

This is also dedicated to all those brave light-workers, empaths, change-makers, and truth-seekers, who are finding the strength within themselves to open-up to possibilities, speak their truth, while stepping out of the spiritual closet.

I'd also like to honor my two brilliant and amazing daughters, Amelia and Nakita Kohan.

(Left, Nakita is a singer / actress, age 25) Nik bought her first house at age 18 and is one of the hardest working script supervisors in the Vancouver Film Industry.

The 2nd pic is Nik at 5-months-old, smiling just after her bath.

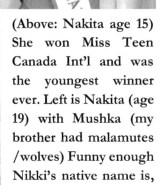

'Girl who speaks with wolves'

(Above: Nakita age 15) She won Miss Teen Canada Int'l and was the youngest winner ever. Left is Nakita (age 19) with Mushka (my brother had malamutes /wolves) Funny enough Nikki's native name is,

173

Below: Amelia is 22 years old. She's a talented actress, model and

singer as well. Now living in Portugal, Amelia is a dental assistant and Elite Lisbon is her Acting Agent. (Middle left: Is

Mother's Day Tea, Amelia Rose age 6 and me 42, (She surprised me with this very special day xo) Left: Amelia and her fiancé Jack – in their family dental clinic.

(Above Right: Amelia won Miss Teen Vancouver and Miss Teen Canada Int'l Fundraiser. Here she is with her sister, just seconds after winning) Both you girls inspired me to return from the Heavens. You are my reasons 'why'. Thank you for agreeing to have me as your Mom - given all we've gone through, know that I love you both so very much. I love you to the moon and back! 🩶

My niece Hannah-Jane is also like a daughter to me. Thank you for coming into our world. You're one of the bravest and strongest, most beautiful young women I know. Love you very much sweetheart! So grateful for you! Love you to the moon and back as well! Xoxoxoxox :D

(Above left: Hannah 2021. Above Right: Hannah and me 2016)

(Above Left: My Mom and newborn baby Hannah-Jane xo)
Above Right: Hannah 3 or 4 months old with her Mom (my sister Cathy) and me at Grandma Dee's house. 🩶

And a huge thank you to my Mountain-man brother... who was my best friend and I loved with every bit of my soul... Tom Byrnell

Tom, you've been my ally and one of my greatest teachers. You've literally saved my life twice! And without you, I wouldn't be here – nor would the girls, and nor would this book.

So, thank you Tom. You were the BEST storyteller, professional cartoonist, and brother I could have ever wished for. You made all those who knew you, laugh uncontrollably with your wit and humor. You were an unassuming Mensa genius who left us far too young. "Watching the History (or Discovery) Channel, just isn't the same without you Joe!" ;) xo

Another great BIG thank you goes to my Best Friends and Soul Sisters who helped get me started. Kelly Woodhouse Falardeau (pic left) and Sher Packolyk (pic below) I love you both! Kelly, together we built courses that helped so many others write their own books, but it also inspired me to start this book once and for all! I am so grateful to you and Kathy Kiss - who were the catalysts here, forcing me to put pen to paper.

And same goes to my longest friend, and likely one of the most gifted psychics that I know, Sher Packolyk (Right). Sher and I worked together for years in the film industry. I was a Casting Director and she was (in my opinion) the Best Agent EVER! Together we helped to create many great shows! Sher is truly my

'Go-to Gal'. She's a psychic's psychic, and has been there for me and my girls every step of the way… I'm so grateful for these ladies in our world, and their amazing advice along the way! Xo ♡

I'd also like to give one of the BIGGEST Thank You's to the rest

of my Soul Pak family, my Mom, Dad, Nana, and sister Cathy. Each of you are such beautiful Souls, and I love you all very much! (Left – was after my Mom´s quadruple bypass surgery at age 42, I quickly learned to cook. I was 12 years old at the time and was so happy in this picture that my Mom was still alive!)

Mom, you were my bestfriend EVER! Like I said to you when you were passing away, "You were one of the finest Souls to ever walk this plane, and it's been a privilege being your daughter." I so miss your laughter and joy! And the eclectic assortment of music we'd loved to listen to full blast, with the windows of the house open, as we'd dance in the kitchen together... So much fun!

(Right: Mom (31), Nana (55), Cathy (6) and me (8 months-ish?) Here, we were living in Northern Quebec on the military base)

Mom, you were such a special woman indeed. You taught me how to parent through your unconditional love, and I strive to see the world through your eyes and heart more every day. ♡

Dad (Right & Below) you were one of the best story tellers, and smartest men I've ever known! You were one of the country's leading Sports-Medicine Experts, Trainers & Physical Therapists. You worked with the LA Kings, and the Edmonton Oilers Hockey Teams. Plus, Team Canada's soccer  (football), hockey, and so many Olympic teams as well. You were inducted into the Sports Hall of Fame, and you were also awarded the Military Merit Medal from the Governor General of Canada.

In hindsight, I believe you were a Medical Intuitive and obviously others thought the same, when they gave you the nickname,

"X-Ray Eyes Byrnell"

And like Mom, you were far ahead of your time - with you being an inventor and pioneer in Sports Medicine.

I was so blessed to have you both as my parents. Thank you to both of you for saying "Yes."

Love you Mom and Dad! ♡

To my sister Cathy. I'm so glad we've healed our relationship. I've missed your humor. You really should be a stand-up comedian. Plus, you're such a talented Artist. Love ya always! So grateful you're my sister. Together, we are proof that love (along with The Five Lessons of Life) definitely heals all. It certainly healed us! Love ya Cath xo Btw, I so look forward to our nightly calls. We laugh till we cry... So much fun!

And finally, I'd like to thank the 3 men who have helped to shape the girl's and my life - both past, present and future.

Thank you to my former husband (Left: with our youngest daughter at her Grad)

I thank you for teaching (and showing me) unconditional love and for marrying (and divorcing) me... I'm grateful we're friends again. And thank you for our two amazing and lovely daughters.

Looking back at the paths we've walked, both side-by-side and apart, I can see Creator truly does have a greater plan for all of us. Especially when he added new loving stepparents and family members into the girl's and our lives. ♡

And to Eric...

Thank you for always being there for us.

(Right: Eric having an unexpected visit with his 'almost daughter' Nakita and me in Toronto, Canada 2018)

I always knew you would do well in life Eric. I'm grateful we've stayed connected through all these years and decades. Much love from the Kohan girls! xo

(Above: 2017 - Lake Louise)
"Being deeply loved by someone gives you strength,
while loving someone deeply gives you courage."
—Lao Tzu

Most of all, I'd like to acknowledge and thank my future husband Lindsay for his support, love, and laughter. I'm grateful that we showed up for one another. What I love about Linds, and our relationship is that we meditate together daily... We love watching UFOs together in the night sky, and you have honored my history and insights and have never called me 'crazy'. Thank you honey... You are the kind, thoughtful, loving, spiritual man whom I prayed for. Thank you for showing up online and bringing me and my girls to Europe. You've changed our worlds completely and I love you so much.

In closing, there were actually four men who helped to sculpt my life... The 4th man is the one who I had the abortion with. He shall remain anonymous because today, his work is well known - as he's working with some of the most famous composers, singers and performers on this planet. Again, I'm so grateful for the directions we both took in life - especially when I look at the families we've both created, and the children we've had in our own lives since parting ways... These children wouldn't have come into this world had we forced our paths to stick together, and not been open to what was to come. I wish my former partner and his family every blessing in the world. Because in the end, love is all we can desire for one another...

In writing this book and reviewing the past 54 years, I'd say I've come to practice 'The 5 Lessons of Life' on more days than not. And after reading or listening to this book, it is my hope that you will do the same.

Warmest Wishes,

Sessions, Retreats & Workshops

Email us for information on Courses and Classes, Workshops, or even Writer´s Retreats - where you´ll be staying in Carrie´s Guesthouse in Portugal (or a Chateau in France perhaps!).

For information on courses and availability, contact us at:

support@carriekohan.com

1993

2nd Death

June 22 - Died; 9D Hologram Review of my Life; Memory Self;

Council of Men; 5LOL; Birthday!

June 18 - Engaged to Michael;

June 11 - Met Michael

June 9 - Met Angel with message; Eric and I agreed to part ways;

June 3 - Stargate 11:11;

1992

1st Death

Broke! Moved into Studiosuite (downstairs); Met with the Devil & Gremlins; God & Jesus; Travelled into the Black Void; 'Woke Up' and moved across the City to the Hippy-Dippy-House

1991

Bartender

Became a Full-blown dysfunctional human being! Bartending at Richards On Richards and Royal Vancouver Yacht Club in Vancouver B.C.;closet alcoholic

1990

Moved Vic-Van

Did the Tony Robbins'Tape program. Sold my 2 properties in Victoria & moved to Vancouver; Rented Penthouse suite; became an Actress

1988

Abortion

1st abortion in VictoriaBC hospital after Premier Van Der Zalm made the procedure legal again.

Boyfriend left me – He lost three people that day

Index

These Pages Are Also For You! Xoxo

It's your turn to put pen to paper... Please write your thoughts & Discussions Notes here... For Self-Development; Teaching Classes; Sermons; Book Club or Toast Masters Talking Points... This is your place to make notes of memorable ideas, insights and inspirations.

Much Love and Light ♡

www.CarrieKohan.com

Made in United States
Troutdale, OR
12/18/2023

16047809R00110